I AM THE EXECUTOR:

WHAT DO I DO?

David J. C. Nicholl

NIMBUS
PUBLISHING

Nimbus Publishing Limited
PO Box 9166,
Halifax, Nova Scotia B3K 5M8
(902) 455-4286

Design: Kate Westphal
Graphic Detail Inc.
Charlottetown, PEI
Cover photo by David Muir

Printed and bound in Canada

Canadian Cataloguing in Publication Data
Nicholl, David J.C., 1925-
I am the executor
ISBN 1-55109-237-9

1. Executors and administrators—Nova Scotia—
popular works.   I. Title.
KEN7648.Z82N52 1999   346.716056
C98-950146-9

Nimbus Publishing acknowledges the financial
support of the Canada Council and the
Department of Canadian Heritage.

To Alice Creighton, my wife and best friend, and to our daughter Linda. This book would not have been written if they had not urged me to give them and my sons, Stuart, Paul, and Peter an easy to understand source of information about executors, wills, estates, and related matters. Alice, Linda, and Peter were very helpful with story format and editing, for which I am very grateful.

Assistance from The Loewen Group Inc. and Cruikshank's Funeral Home in Nova Scotia is also acknowledged.

TABLE OF CONTENTS

INTRODUCTION

There really is no great mystery about the process and duties of an executor ("liquidator," in Quebec; "estate trustee," in Ontario). People from all walks of life have been settling estates for centuries. All it takes is some time and effort, integrity, and an understanding of the position's responsibilities and duties, which are the same for the smallest of estates as they are for those valued in millions of dollars. Once an executor understands his or her responsibilities, fulfilling them can be a relatively simple and straightforward process.

While courts issue documents detailing some of the legal duties and responsibilities of executors, they contain little "how to" information. No guidance is given on just how one goes about gathering and assembling estate-related documents, preparing lists of assets for inventory valuation, setting up a bookkeeping system, opening the estate's bank account, knowing what income tax returns have to be prepared and filed, and getting a tax clearance certificate from Revenue Canada. There are other things, too, that executors have to do, such as placing advertisements in specific publications to notify interested parties that an estate is being "opened."

Everyone making a will appoints one or more people, or an institution, to be the executor(s) of his or her estate. Except in Quebec, the appointment is legally confirmed by the process of proving in a court that it is truly the last will made by the deceased. In the majority of cases, the proving process is not a difficult one, and the laws are designed to handle virtually every unusual circumstance, such as when witnesses to the will are dead. When an executor's appointment has been confirmed by a probate court, he or she has two options concerning distributing the remaining assets and closing the estate. These are commonly referred to as formal and informal closings. The formal process requires that a full accounting of the executor's steward-ship be presented and accepted by the probate court which confirmed the appointment. An informal closing can be done, where permitted by provincial or territorial laws, by the executor simply distributing all remaining assets without presenting an accounting to the probate court. The advantage of an informal closing is not having to pay additional fees to the court.

When either process has been fully and correctly completed, the executor's work is finished. However, it is generally considered preferable to have court records show that an estate was formally closed and all legalities fulfilled. The latter course provides the executor with virtual immunity from responsibility for any claims made by disgruntled relatives of the deceased, or anyone else. On the other hand, for example, in estates where the spouse of the deceased is both the executor and residual beneficiary, there is generally no need to incur the expense of a formal closing. (See chapter 15 for more information on formal and informal closings.)

This book has been written to assist new and even semi-experienced executors along the do-it-yourself trail. It contains the step-by-step case history of how Mary Fraser, an imaginary character, administered her husband's estate following his sudden death. She kept costs to a minimum by using professional help only when needed. The case is fictional; the process and documents are not.

Copies of legal and court documents are provided together with an explanation and description of the purpose of each one, along with a list of the files Mary set up to keep her papers and documents in an easy, systematic order for quick reference.

Topics covered are:

• Mary's going to court to have the will probated and to be appointed executrix;

• The simple accounting records she kept, from the opening of the estate until its closing and final disbursements;

• Her decision when to have an accountant prepare a summary for the court from her listings of money received and spent, and income tax returns;

• Her keeping complete control over all assets right from the start. Mary did not have to ask someone else where estate matters stood because she knew herself;

• Her limiting the lawyer's role.

If called upon to be an executrix again, Mary would prepare all documents required by the registrar of probate herself and use a lawyer only to take her affidavit on those papers which had to be signed under oath. The copy of the Probate Act she had obtained contains many of the basic forms needed, and the registrar's office readily gave documentation guidance. As it was, by Mary's keeping lawyer services to a minimum, legal expenses were below $800.

Many financial institutions and other organizations publish promotional pamphlets concerning wills and estates. While they contain some information about being an executor and executorship duties, none contain complete case histories with copies of actual documents. This book fills that gap.

Although the setting for the case history is the County of Halifax, Nova Scotia, the process of probating a will is basically the same in all provinces and territories. The first step is to have the deceased's last will and a document recording date of death presented to a probate court in the jurisdiction where the deceased had residence. When the court is satisfied the will is valid, the deceased's appointment of the surviving executor(s) is confirmed. The executor then has documentary proof of legal authority to act for and administer the estate by carrying out the instructions contained in the will.

Each province and territory in Canada has its own civil laws dealing with wills, estates, guardianships, intestacies, the age of majority, power of attorney, living wills, and similar matters. These topics are discussed in chapter 11, and the addresses of places where copies of applicable acts can be obtained are also supplied. While it may be necessary in some jurisdictions to use the services of a lawyer to prepare most or even all documents required for presentation to probate courts,

executors can reduce legal costs by doing all of the estate administration and distributions themselves. After all, it is the executor, not someone else, who is responsible for fulfilling executorship responsibilities. Some acts contain draft copies of documents the courts require, making it easy for anyone to prepare them for use in presentations to probate courts. If the court finds that these documents are not exactly in the desired format, any changes can easily be made and the documents resubmitted. Probate personnel and registrars are frequently able and willing to provide executors with explanations about court procedures and document requirements, which is particularly helpful to novice executors.

The information and opinions expressed in this book are not intended to be a substitute for legal advice. Provincial and territorial acts applicable to wills, administration of estates, powers of attorney, guardianships, and so on, recognize that other civil laws can come into play in some circumstances, such as insanity, spousal matrimonial rights, or divorce. Disgruntled relatives and others sometimes contest the provisions of wills and division of assets contending they are not receiving what they believe they should. When executors are confronted with any problems with possible legal implications it is imperative that legal advice be obtained. Legal fees are paid by the estate. Each province and territory has its own statutes dealing with civil matters, including estates; Revenue Canada's reporting and filing regulations are the same in all jurisdictions.

In this book, words importing any one gender are to be understood to include the other gender. The words executor and executrix are interchangeable wherever they occur.

Following chapter 11 are various comments and information about wills, including topics such as dying without having made a will, contesting wills, small estates, bankrupt estates, executors, guardianships, powers of attorney, and living wills, as well as formal and informal estate closings.

David J. C. Nicholl

I

JAMES FRASER
DIES UNEXPECTEDLY

The Frasers had lived in a house on Crichton Avenue, Dartmouth, Nova Scotia since they were married in 1959. James, a Dalhousie University graduate, had found a job with the telephone company; he liked his work, and it turned out to be his lifelong employment. Although they seldom discussed it, he planned to retire in 1999 at the age of 65. His wife, Mary, three years younger, had been working at the *Dartmouth Free Press* when they married, and carried on there until the birth of their first child, Elizabeth Jane. Christopher Robert was born three years later. Elizabeth was married to Charles Wilson and had two children, Joanne, in 1990, and Stanley, in 1992. Christopher did not marry.

When the children were quite young James and Mary had bought a seaside cottage in Chester Basin, about an hour's drive from Dartmouth. They had two cars, both registered in James's name. Their parents were deceased and had left them some money. James had invested his with a stockbroker, and Mary had put hers in a bank. Each had a safety deposit box, but in different banks. His bank was close to his office in Halifax and hers was close to home in a shopping mall.

While they had intended to sign bank forms giving them access to each others' boxes, the joint access document to James's box was never completed. It had been mislaid and forgotten.

James was a keen golfer, playing at Chester's semi-private course when staying at the cottage in Chester Basin, and at the Brightwood Golf and Country Club when living at home. He had memberships in both. On May 24, 1996, he suffered a heart attack on the Dartmouth course. He died in hospital shortly thereafter with his doctor in attendance. Dr. Reuben Offman promptly went to the family home on Crichton Avenue with the sad news. Needless to say, Mary and the children were in shock and completely devastated.

Gently, Dr. Offman told Mary that the hospital was waiting to release Jim's body to a funeral home as soon as it could be arranged. He then added that unless she or Jim had made arrangements with a funeral home, she or his executor would now have to pick one.

Mary replied that she was his executor, but didn't know which funeral home to choose. "Let me think about it and phone you within an hour or so," she said. Mary knew she was Jim's executor because they had named each other as their executors in their wills. He had kept a photocopy of his will with his bank statements and other papers in a desk at his office. She kept a photocopy of hers in the drawer of her writing desk.

In Mary's state of shock it was very difficult for her to make decisions about anything. Neighbourhood news travels quickly, and soon her next-door neighbour and friend Ruby arrived. Ruby told the doctor she would help Mary select a funeral home. Ruby had lost her first husband three years ago, and knew what was involved in arranging a funeral. The first thing to be decided was the type of funeral. After the type was determined it would be important to get a competitive price as prices can vary between funeral homes.

The doctor told Mary he needed some additional family information to complete the death certificate. Provincial government forms required the surnames, given names, and birthplaces of James's parents; James's social insurance number; the date and place of his birth; all his given names; his occupation; and Mary's full maiden name. Dr. Offman also asked if Jim's driver's license recorded him as an organ donor. Struggling hard for control and to remember names and dates, Mary went to the bedroom and found Jim's wallet. In it was his social insurance card and his driver's license with the word "DONOR" printed on it in red letters.

After receiving the information he needed, the doctor returned to the hospital to contact the organ donor registry and complete the death certificate. The hospital needed to have the doctor's certificate, showing cause of death, to complete their records before they would release the body to a funeral home. If any of Jim's organs could be used by the donor bank, they would be surgically removed before the body left the hospital. On its release the funeral home would have to get a burial permit from the province. For Jim there was no reason to expect any delay by the coroner's

office in issuing the permit once it received Dr. Offman's death report. His death had occurred in the hospital and its cause was clear, particularly as the doctor had told Jim several times that his blood pressure was higher than it should be. An autopsy would not be required.*

During his visit Dr. Offman had also explained to Mary the process of identifying the body of the deceased. The normal procedure is that the widow or some other member of the immediate family identifies the body. This is usually done at the mortuary rather than the hospital, because many people are not in hospitals when they die.

Before going home to contact local funeral service providers Ruby asked Mary if she and Jim had discussed or put in writing the kind of funeral arrangements they would have liked for themselves. Mary responded that they had seldom talked about their own funerals, and that when they did, Jim had seemed to favour what he called "traditional" funeral services, like those of his parents. The family had had an evening visitation at the funeral home and a church service, followed by burial in a cemetery. Mary and Jim had on occasion briefly discussed cremation for themselves as being more practicable and economical. Occasionally they had talked about selecting a funeral home and making arrangements for their funerals, but they kept putting off actually doing it or recording any preferences. Also, like many people, they did not own a burial plot. Mary realized now that unless they wanted to be cremated, they should have bought a cemetery plot, preferably somewhere nearby. On the other hand, if Jim were to be cremated, it would not be urgent to decide where he would be interred.

---

* When someone dies elsewhere than in a hospital, the coroner is more likely to require an autopsy report before granting a burial permit. Exceptions are made if the deceased has been under a medical doctor's care, or has died from natural causes, such as old age, protracted illness, and so on. Burial or cremation cannot take place until the coroner's office issues a permit.

Ruby went home and phoned three local funeral homes. The funeral directors all told Ruby that their prices were based on the number and extent of services they were asked to provide. Prices did not include the cost of caskets, urns, opening and closing the grave, cremation, catering, clergy and organist fees as well as some other items. The task was more difficult than Ruby had expected, but she was able to get a range of approximate prices, all dependent on the extent of services requested. There were four main types of funerals offered:

1. Traditional Service; full package

The kind that Jim's parents had with the body being embalmed and placed in a coffin for viewing at the funeral home, including visitations there by family and friends, coffee and tea provided, a guest book for signatures, acknowledgement cards and envelopes, limousine service for family and clergy, a church service, a reception at the church after the service, and interment in a cemetery. $3,500 and up, according to the extent of services requested.

2. Traditional Service; partial package

The same as the first option, but without a church service; the package includes a reception at the funeral home, a religious service in the home's chapel, refreshments and limo service, or any variations of these. $3,100 and up, according to the extent of service requested.

3. Memorial Service; with visitation and church service

Cremation, an urn in a room at the funeral home, visitations there by family and friends, tea and coffee provided, a guest book for signatures, acknowledgement cards and

envelopes, limousine service for family and clergy, and a church service and reception afterwards. Graveside urn burial service was also included. $2,700 and up, according to the extent of services requested.

4. Cremation Services; basic professional services only

Transfer from the place of death to the funeral home and the crematorium. The package offered the choice of graveside urn burial or having the urn released to the family. $1,440 for having the body cremated with the ashes (which weigh six to ten pounds) given to the family. Cemetery plots cost $150, with an opening and closing charge of $90. The cost of urns ranged from $400 to $2,000.

The prices did not include applicable sales tax.

In the process of gathering this information Ruby was favourably impressed with Mr. Kirk Orde, the director of City Funeral Home Ltd. He, like the other two funeral directors, suggested the best procedure would be for the Frasers to come to his office, where he could further explain and discuss services and prices. In view of the emotional strains the Frasers were under, he said, he would be pleased to come to their home to help them decide which services they would like to have provided. Mr. Orde also described the many items to be dealt with in planning a funeral, such as making church service and reception arrangements, getting the obituary to the newspapers, contacting pall bearers, and so on. Ruby thanked him and said she would give him a call after talking to Mrs. Fraser.

Ruby returned to Mary's with her information and suggested that Mr. Orde be invited to come to 937 Crichton Avenue as soon as possible. Mary had attended a service in City Funeral Home several years before, when one of Jim's friends had died, and felt it would be acceptable. While she really did not want to have any strangers in the house just then to add to the confusion, there seemed to be no better way than to have him come to them. Ruby phoned Mr. Orde, and, while waiting for him to arrive, Mary, her son, her daughter, and Ruby reviewed the cost figures for the various types of burial. Although a memorial cremation service would be more economical and less stressful, they decided to have a traditional full-package funeral in keeping with what Jim had wanted. They would try to keep costs down wherever it seemed appropriate to do so.

When Mr. Orde arrived, the Frasers described to him the service they wanted. It was decided to have a visitation at the funeral home the following evening; a service at the family's church the day after that, preferably at 2:30 in the afternoon; and burial in a cemetery. Mr. Orde had brought copies of City Funeral Home's working file (Exhibit No. 1) used to record virtually all the information and data required for a funeral. He distributed copies to the family and by the time he had filled in the first page, decisions on most of the other details had been made and he could complete the costs section on page 3. He explained the various services provided by the funeral home and gave their prices:

- Fee for professional services, including charges for staff at visitation receptions at the funeral home, services at the church, looking after all documentation and providing funeral stationary: $1,500

- Care and preparation of the deceased, including dressing and makeup: 400

- Use of funeral home facilities and equipment for the reception, and holding room and reception service: 575

- Automotive equipment to transport the body from the hospital to the home and deliver necessary cemetery equipment, a limousine for the family, and a funeral coach: 400

- Family wreath, to be placed on the casket: 75

TOTAL   **$2,950**

There would also be fees for clergy and organist honorariums, grave opening and closing fees, the casket enclosure box and the casket itself.

Concerning the need to acquire a cemetery plot, Mr. Orde said he could look after having the estate purchase one in Sackville Cemetery. It was presently selling two-person lots for $1,500, which included perpetual care, but it did not have any single lots for sale at the present time. Elizabeth and Chris both agreed with Mary's plan to use Mr. Orde's services and to bury their father in the Sackville cemetery.

Mr. Orde then explained that it would be necessary for some member of the family to come to the funeral home to identify the body and choose the casket. Also, as soon as possible, he said, they should prepare an obituary which could be given to him either over the phone or in writing. He would, he added, look after giving it to the newspaper, and reminded the Frasers that he would need the names and phone numbers of four pallbearers. Before he left Mary and Chris decided it would suit them best to go to the funeral home late in the afternoon at about four o'clock. Mr. Orde agreed that would be a good time for him.

Elizabeth found her dad's Brightwood Golf Club membership booklet and phoned the three other members of his regular foursome, asking them if they would be pall bearers. All agreed, and she told them someone from the funeral home would be contacting them. Then she phoned Jim's office and gave his closest friend there the sad news. He agreed to be the fourth pall bearer, and offered to help the funeral director if required. Elizabeth wrote the names of the four men and their home and business phone numbers on a piece of paper, for her mother and Chris to give to Mr. Orde. She did not feel up to going with them, and stayed in the house until they returned.

Chris said he would write a draft obituary for his mother and sister to read and edit. He had never written one before and looked at some in the morning newspaper for general format. What he wrote had Jim's full name and age; the names of his father, mother, and predeceased sister, as well as those of Mary, Elizabeth, and himself, and the grandchildren; the funeral home visitation date and time; the church service date and time; and the place of interment. After making a few little changes and adding "family flowers only" and "donations to the Dartmouth Heart and Stroke Foundation or any charity," his mother and sister agreed it was okay. Christopher phoned Mr. Orde and read it to him. He said it was just fine and he would look after giving it to the newspapers.

In the meantime Rev. Harry Cleves, the minister at Woodside United Church, phoned to confirm he had been contacted by Mr. Orde. The service, he said, was scheduled for 2:30 P.M. on the 26th, and the Ladies' Auxiliary had arranged to serve coffee, tea, sandwiches, and cookies in the church hall after the service. He added that the choir would attend, and that he had obtained copies of the late Dr. Helen Creighton's "Hills and Glens," which had been sung at her own funeral. The words were to be included in the pamphlet being prepared for the service, for sidesmen to give to the congregation as they enter the church.

At four o'clock, Chris took Mary to the funeral home to formally identify Jim's body. Fortunately, she had taken two of the tranquillizer tablets Dr. Offman had given her, because seeing the body was such a shock that even as it was she would

have collapsed to the floor if Chris had not had his arm around her to keep her from falling. They returned to Mr. Orde's office and sat for a few minutes before going with him to the casket showroom, where at least thirty coffins were displayed. All their lids were up to show interiors, and attached to each one was a card with a brief description and price. Mr. Orde walked slowly with them through the display, and before returning to his office, asked Mary and Chris to come to him if they had any questions. Left by themselves, they felt free to discuss appearances and prices without any influence from the director, which might have made them feel uncomfortable. With prices ranging from $995 to $9,645, they decided to concentrate first on the appearances of caskets priced below $2,500. They eventually narrowed the choice down to a grey cloth-covered wood casket priced at $1,360 and returned to Mr. Orde's office.

With their having chosen the casket, Mr. Orde could now complete the listing of costs, including clergy and organist payments, cemetery costs, and the family wreath. The total, including HST, came to $5,566.50. Mr. Orde made a photocopy of page 3 of the funeral home's working file, which contained cost details, and handed it to Chris. Chris signed on page 4 of the document to record that he had identified the body, and signed again for receiving his father's watch, clothes, wedding ring, and $2.74 in loose change. He agreed to return within an hour or two with one of Jim's suits, a shirt, and a tie. Mary was too exhausted to talk on the way back home.

Sad news travels fast. Friends, neighbours, relatives, and Jim's co-workers were quick to come to the Fraser home, bringing food and offering to do whatever they could to help the family through its shock and grief. Fortunately, there was no immediate financial concern, since Mary had enough money in her chequing account to take care of any expenses that had to be paid right away.

Anything else could be taken care of in a couple of weeks. Funeral costs would be paid by the estate when banking arrangements had been made.

Next evening was an emotional time for everyone as they came to the funeral home for visitation. The family's decision to have the casket closed helped many mourners relax a bit and stay longer.

The following afternoon most of the pews at Woodside United Church were filled with relatives, golf club members, friends, and business associates. During the service Rev. Cleves announced that the Frasers were inviting everyone to join them downstairs for refreshments. He added that the family would be going to Sackville Cemetery, but would be back to be with them following the interment. Nearly half the congregation went to the cemetery. Most of these came back with the Frasers.

Receiving condolences and chatting with friends and acquaintances from near and far in the more relaxed atmosphere of the church helped lessen their shock and despair; none the less it was a very long, difficult day for Mary and the whole Fraser family.

II

MARY FRASER, THE EXECUTOR, STARTS GATHERING DATA

Mary soon found that the letters of condolence and sympathy cards she received, as well as the donations in James's memory to the Heart and Stroke Foundation, were all helping her through her grieving process, a period during which she would build the strength she needed now to face living alone. Nearly a week went by before she had caught up and mailed the last acknowledgement.

Finally she felt ready to deal with financial matters and tackle being executor of James's estate. A few years earlier, Jim and Mary had given considerable thought about who they should have as executors. Both felt the most important people to be involved in each other's estate were themselves, followed by the children. Without having any deep discussions with Elizabeth and Chris, they had decided to put common disaster clauses (see glossary) in their wills, making the children co-executors in the event neither of them could be executor for one another. Mary and Jim were not secretive and each had a fairly good idea of the other's assets. He had a greater amount of business and administrative experience than she, but Mary had gained some understanding of what an

executor has to do when her parents had died. With the confidence of knowing professional help could be obtained if and when needed, Jim and Mary had agreed to make and accept each other's appointment as executors.

Mary was an energetic person. Over the past few days she had decided just where she should begin. She started with a "to do" list of important things she must do without further delay:

1. ***Get Jim's original will from his safety deposit box with the Bank of Montreal, George Street, Halifax.*** (Her photocopy would not be accepted for probate, and to transact business in the name of Jim's estate, she would need to have the will probated.)

2. ***Six proof of death certificates from City Funeral Home.*** (Six should be enough, and if necessary Mary could get more from them. To get them from the province's Vital Statistics Office would take a couple of weeks. These certificates would be needed to collect on insurance policies, probate the will, and get into Jim's box at the bank. Also, Health and Welfare

would want one for the Canada Pension Plan and other copies would probably be needed elsewhere).

3. **Gather all Jim's recent bank account statements and passbooks, his investment and income statements from the broker, his tax returns for 1993, 1994, and 1995, his RRSP reports, payroll statements, life insurance policies, car and property insurance policies, car registrations, and information on any other assets, as well as any bills he may owe. Check for insurance coverage on his Mastercard account.** (Their mortgage was life insured but it was paid off five years ago.)

4. **Contact Jim's office and arrange to have all personal mail they may receive forwarded to me.**

5. **Make a preliminary list of Jim's assets.** (Estimated values were all that are needed to get the will probated.)

6. **Contact Canada Pension Plan office for their information.**

7. **Find out what types of memorial stones can be put in Sackville Cemetery.**

8. **Get two people to appraise Jim's estate's inventory when it is completed.** (The probate court required it.) **Maybe my bank manager and Chris's accountant friend will do it.**

9. **Get a lawyer to prepare whatever documents I initially need to take to probate court to be officially appointed executor.** (Mary wanted to do whatever she could herself, and would ask the lawyer to tell her which documents she could look after, and which ones he should prepare. She wanted to keep legal costs to a minimum while she learned the whole process of what an executor must and should do. She had heard staff at the registrar's office were helpful to new executors.)

10. **Get a copy of the province's Probate Act from the government bookstore.**

11. **Set up a separate filing system for estate documents, letters, money received, expenses, receipts, tax returns, and so on.**

Next morning Mary drove across the bridge to Halifax, to the Bank of Montreal where Jim had banked. When she presented the key to James's safety deposit box, she was informed that since her name was not on the rental agreement she could not have access to it. However, when she showed a proof of death certificate a bank employee opened it for her. Because James had not had her name added to the rental agreement, which would had given her unrestricted access, the bank attendant stood by while Mary briefly examined the box's contents and took out Jim's will, headed Last Will And Testament (exhibit no. 2). The attendant examined the will to confirm that it appointed Mary Ann Fraser as executor and permitted her to remove only it, then waited while Mary looked through the rest of the contents. The attendant made a copy of the proof of death for the bank's records, returned the original to Mary, then placed a seal on the box, indicating the lessee was deceased. Mary would not be permitted to remove the contents of the box until officially appointed executrix by the Court of Probate. During her brief examination of the contents Mary wrote in her notebook that it contained $25,000 in Canada Savings Bonds, 1,000 shares in the Bank of Nova Scotia; 500 shares in Air

Canada; 1,000 shares in Nova Scotia Power; a $25,000 Maritime Life insurance policy and a $10,000 Canada Life insurance policy, both naming her as beneficiary; several old stock certificates with unfamiliar names; and envelopes containing old stamps and coins.

Mary returned home with the original will. It was dated November 25, 1993, and had been witnessed by neighbours Glenn and Elizabeth Holmes, who had moved to Amherst two years ago. Fortunately they had seen James's obituary in the newspaper and in addition to sending a donation, Elizabeth had written to Mary, so she had their current address. She phoned the Holmeses to find out which one of them would sign the legal document needed to prove to the Court of Probate that the will was actually signed by Jim and in their presence. Glenn said he would gladly do it and just needed to know where and when.

Jim's and Mary's wills had been prepared for them by Jim's uncle Charlie, who had since moved to California. A lot of thought and planning had been done before the wills were typed, on two legal-size (14-inch-long) pages. (This is the size generally used by lawyers, but paper size is actually of no importance for wills.) Paragraphs not ending at the right-hand side of the page used a series of periods reaching to the side, to fill any blank spaces, a common practice to eliminate the risk of anyone's making an insertion after a will has been signed. From their discussions back in 1993, Mary knew what Jim had intended in his will. The only difficult decision had been what to do with the cottage. Mary had not wanted to be left with the responsibility of its care, maintenance, upkeep, taxes, and operating expenses. On the other hand, she had wanted to be able to continue having unrestricted use of it. To keep ownership in the family, it had been decided that Jim should leave it to one or both of the children. When they discussed what to do with the cottage

with Chris and Elizabeth, Elizabeth had said that she and Charles were buying a cottage lot at Cow Bay and did not want to be responsible for sharing the expenses of the Chester Basin property. So in his will, Jim had given it to Chris, with Mary to have full unrestricted use of it until her death. Jim's will stipulated that $500 donations be given to the church and to the Rotary Club; their newest car, now a Buick, be given to Mary; and the older car to daughter Elizabeth. In addition to bequests of $5,000 to each grandchild, Jim had directed that the residue of his estate be divided, half to Mary and the other half split equally between Elizabeth and Christopher. This made the three of them the residual beneficiaries, sharing what would be left in the estate after all debts, gifts, taxes, and expenses were paid. In with the will was a note in Jim's handwriting saying that Christopher was to have his golf clubs and hunting rifle.

Mary took the will to MicMac Shopping Mall and made three photocopies, one for herself, one for Elizabeth, and one for Christopher. The original would end up in probate court. She gave the children a call, and that evening they read the will and talked about what had to be done. The family had always been close, and Mary assured her children that she would keep them informed about all estate matters and would welcome suggestions and answer any questions they might have as best she could. However, she also told them that, in her position as executrix, she had sole responsibility for administrating the estate in accordance with the terms of the will.

Both said they understood this and appreciated her desire to keep them informed, which, they agreed, was the best way to avoid misunderstandings. Mary had heard of family disputes and even break-ups which had taken years to overcome just because good lines of communication had not been established at the start. She was not going to let this happen to her family. (Residual beneficiaries are stakeholders in an estate because they will share in the final distribution of whatever is left after all specific gifts, taxes, debts, and estate fees have been paid. This gives them every right to know how the executor is progressing toward having the estate settled and distributing residue to them.)

The government's Canada Pension Plan office was listed in the phone book under Human Resources Development Canada—CPP. Mary called the CPP office for the forms which needed to be filed besides a proof of death, and James's and Mary's birth and marriage certificates. The only additional document required was a letter from Jim's employer stating the amounts of his CPP contributions in 1996. Jim's company sent the letter to Mary, and she sent it and the other items to the CPP office. Jim had paid the full amount of CPP premiums for many years, but even so Mary was surprised when she received a death payment cheque for $3,540, payable to the estate, with a notice she would immediately begin receiving a portion of James's CPP retirement entitlement. The notice included a form for her to complete if she wanted the money deposited directly into her bank account. The amount would be $399 a month until her 65th birthday, and then increase to $436. Her Canada Pension Plan survivor entitlements took into account both James's and Mary's ages, his contribution amounts, and the number of years he had contributed. Mary was told that the calculations were complicated and the entitlements not the same for everyone. A week later a letter arrived, returning the proof of death and their birth and marriage certificates.

When Mary asked her Bank of Nova Scotia manager to be an inventory appraiser he agreed. She made a phone call to Christopher's accounting friend, Peter Wilford, and he also agreed to be an appraiser. That gave her two responsible people to propose to the registrar of probate to be appraisers of Jim's estate's inventory.

A call to James's supervisor at the phone company assured her that any personal mail would be forwarded to her, as well as papers for filing a claim under the company's group life insurance plan. She was the beneficiary and the amount would be $125,000. The insurance company required a proof of death and marriage certificate, which would also be used to have the phone company's pension plan start making pension payments to Mary. She supplied the documents to the company's personnel officer and asked that the marriage certificate be returned. It was a few days later.

Next to do on her list was to pick a lawyer, set up a filing system, and make a preliminary inventory of Jim's assets. Through her church activities, Mary knew a lawyer whose office was nearby, on Ochterloney Street. She made an appointment for 3:00 P.M. next afternoon. He said an estimated value of James's assets would be needed. By now she had a rough idea of what they were, and promised to supply the lawyer with a list.

Mary wanted to learn all she could about being an executor. In the telephone book under the blue provincial government department pages she found a listing for the government bookstore on Granville Street. The clerk there showed her a copy of the province's Probate Act. It contained legal details about probate and document forms. After scanning it, she concluded it would definitely help her understand some of the processes she would have to go through as the legally appointed executrix of Jim's estate.

Mary knew that the best way to sort and save estate-related information papers as they came along, and have them available for easy reference, was to set up a filing system. She picked up a package of legal size file folders and a cardboard storage box from an office supplies store. Now she had a place to put the estate letters and papers which had been temporarily placed in piles on the dining room table along with other papers found in Jim's desk. The labels she put on folders, which she then placed alphabetically in the box, were:

- Bank of Montreal, Jim's accounts
- Bank of Nova Scotia, estate account
- Cars: Buick and Honda
- Cottage in Chester Basin
- Crichton Avenue residence
- Credit cards
- Disbursement letters and receipts
- Income tax returns for December 31, 1994 and 1995
- Income tax return for May 24, 1996
- Income tax returns for estate
- Inventory May 24, 1996
- Investments
- Life insurance policy claims
- Miscellaneous
- Monument for cemetery
- Pension plans, CPP and company's
- Proof of death forms
- Probate court documents
- Will

The task of listing presently known assets and assigning a *low* estimated value to each was now easier to do. (Low estimated values are used because probate fees are based on inventory value. The court adjusts its fee when an exact inventory valuation is presented to it within the required three months. By then the value of all assets should be known, and if not the court can grant an extension.) There was no need for Mary to have to pay a larger estate "opening" fee than necessary. She prepared a list and used values she knew were reasonable, but not overstated:

• Bank of Montreal, chequing account	$3,675
• Savings account	13,621
• GIC due Nov. 6, 1996	15,000
• RRSP	185,500
• 1995 Buick	15,000
• 1991 Honda	4,000
• 1,000 shs Bank of Nova Scotia	30,000
• 500 shs Air Canada	2,000
• 1,000 shs Nova Scotia Power	11,000
• Canada Savings Bonds	25,000
• Cottage, Chester Basin assessed at	43,000
• Stocks with broker, their latest statement	127,311
• Company group life insurance	125,000
• Other Life insurance policies	35,000
TOTAL	**$635,107**

The next day at 3:00 P.M. Mary saw her new lawyer, Mr. Richard Clarke, in his office. She gave him the will and a list of James's assets. Clarke questioned various items: Were bank accounts, home, and cottage in both of their names? Mary replied that their home and savings account were in both, but the cottage was just in Jim's name. Who was the beneficiary of James's life insurance? "I am, and also of the RRSPs," Mary said. Where did the witnesses live and which one would sign to prove the will? Mary told him they now lived in Amherst, where Glenn Holmes would sign any papers required. Clarke informed her that as the Fraser home was partly in her name as a joint tenant, it was not part of the estate, and title to it automatically passed to her. The same was true for the joint account with the Bank of Montreal. The life insurance policies and RRSPs, also, did not form part of the estate assets, since she was their beneficiary. Mary told him her list did not include some things, like Jim's gun and golf clubs, which he had wanted Chris to have; and his clothing, watch, wedding ring, and other personal possessions. Clarke responded that as long as they did not have noteworthy monetary value, and the beneficiaries did not disagree about who she gave them to, such items were almost never included in an estate inventory. Perhaps if she were a professional executrix, he said, she would include everything in the inventory, but even trust companies, when acting as executors, seldom get into dealing with such things unless they are readily convertible to cash.

After Clarke looked over Mary's list, he deducted the items not part of the estate. He subtracted the savings account, the RRSPs, and the two life insurance policies ($13,621, $185,500, $125,000, and $35,000) which reduced the total to $275,986. For the probate court, he divided the new list into "Personal Property" (everything except the cottage) and "Real Property," rounding the number for Personal Property to $236,000 and keeping the cottage's tax assessment value of $43,000 as the value of "Real Property." During a discussion of the services he could provide, Mary explained she planned to look after everything she could on her own, and to seek advice on procedural matters and any problems she might run into. Primarily, she wanted Clarke to prepare the documents she needed to have the legal authority to carry out the instructions in Jim's will. She did not want Clarke to collect and hold estate funds in his lawyer trust account, make the disbursements, or manage the estate—she knew that would be costly. Clarke explained that her first step would be to gain authority over all estate assets by asking the Court of Probate to declare her the legally appointed executrix. Several documents needed to be prepared for her to do this. He agreed to have them ready for her signature in two days.

IV

GOING TO COURT TO BE APPOINTED EXECUTOR

When Mary returned to his office, Richard Clarke had several documents ready for her. The first was an Oath of Executor (exhibit no. 3), in which she swore she believed the will to be true, original, and the last one James had made. Next was the Petition for Probate (exhibit nos. 4A, 4B) a two-part form in which the inventory values of $236,000 and $43,000 were given. She signed in three places. The final item, the Affidavit of Witness (exhibit no. 5) had Mary's former neighbour Glenn Holmes' name typed on it. Clarke explained that registrars of probate require witnesses to sign and swear the affidavit before a judge or registrar of probate, deputy registrar of probate, or such other person as authorized by the Court of Probate. The document, he continued, was prepared for the registrar's use and it would probably be sent to the probate court registrar in Amherst where Holmes could be sworn and sign it. Clarke put the package of documents in a large envelope for Mary along with photocopies for her records. She thanked him and asked that he send his bill for services to date.

At home, Mary addressed a letter to the Registrar, Probate Court (exhibit no. 6) which she would deliver with the documents received from Clarke. Contained in her letter were the names and addresses of the witnesses to the will and the names and addresses of the two appraisers.

The next morning she handed the package to the registrar's staff and told them that if they required any additional information she would be pleased to supply it. Mary explained that she had obtained a copy of the Probate Act and wanted to learn all she could about the process of administrating an estate and would appreciate any advice they could give her. The staff said they would be pleased to tell her about the documents required, but that any lawyer she may have hired would also be able to do this.

Eleven days later Mary received a phone call from the registrar's office who stated that probate had been granted to her under date of June 20, which was the date it had received the completed Affidavit of Witness executed by Mr. Holmes. Once she paid the $1,050 probate fee, she was told, she could pick up the documents at the office. Mary did not have that much money in her own bank account, so she withdrew it from the Frasers' joint savings account at the Bank of Montreal, proceeded to the registrar's office, paid the $1,050, and got a receipt and the probate documents. These were: one Certificate of Probate (exhibit no. 7); six certified copies of probate (exhibit no. 8); two Letters Testamentary (exhibit no. 9) with copy of will attached. The package also included a two-part Warrant of Appraisement (exhibit nos. 10A and 10B) appointing Louis Belliveau and Peter Wilford as the appraisers.

Examining the documents, Mary was puzzled by the fact that the six certified copies of probate were exact copies of the Certificate of Probate except that instead of the registrar's signature, the six copies had the court's stamp on it. When she asked for an explanation she was told that she would get only one certificate, which was not replaceable and should be carefully retained. Additional certified copies could be obtained if she needed more to give to institutions requiring proof that she was executrix of the estate. The two-part Warrant of Appraisement's wording required the executor and appraisers to have the document completed and returned to the registrar within three months. "I have until September 20 to get it done but would like to get it there well before then," Mary told herself.

As she was leaving, one of the registry staff reminded Mary that she would have to arrange to have the estate advertised in the *Royal Gazette*, and gave her the address. The *Gazette* is published weekly, by the authority of the province, to record orders in council, partnership registrations, estate notices, incorporation of new companies, and so on. The purpose of Mary's advertisement would be to make public a legal notification that the estate had been opened, and to supply anyone interested in it with a means of contacting her. The next day Mary delivered a letter to the *Gazette* (exhibit no. 11) with the information needed for the advertisement. She had a certified copy of probate with her which confirmed that probate had been granted

and that Mary had been appointed executrix. She paid the $32.10 publication cost and would recover it when the bank account was opened. A week later a copy of the *Royal Gazette* arrived in the mail with the estate notice (exhibit no. 12) correctly listed. Her notice would appear weekly for six months.

That evening Mary brought Elizabeth and Christopher up-to-date on what she had done so far. Naturally they were very interested in receiving the information about their father's estate. Arrangements to transfer ownership of the cars to Elizabeth and Mary, they agreed, would not be a problem; but the cottage was a different matter. It would go to Christopher, with Mary continuing to use it as she had done before Jim's death. Christopher said he understood that by acquiring ownership of the cottage he would be accepting responsibility for paying all of the bills for it. He and Mary both agreed that they needed to give the matter more thought and should have some sort of written understanding. When Elizabeth and Chris left for home they were satisfied that their mother was making good progress with the estate and felt they soon would be able determine how much their 25 per cent interests would amount to.

Mary had been instructed to keep a complete record of all estate financial transactions, and the time had now come for her to set up a bank account for the estate. She had been a customer of Scotiabank's MicMac Mall branch for many years and the staff knew her well. Taking one of her certified copies of probate to the bank she told them she wanted to open an estate account, on which she could write cheques and earn interest on daily balances. The bank's customer services officer explained the various types of accounts available, and after further discussion it was agreed that there was no need to incur extra service charges by having cancelled cheques returned with her monthly statements. In the unlikely event that Mary needed to prove payments had been made, she should be able to get individual cheques, or photocopies of them, from the bank. She chose the bank's "Basic Banking Savings Account" because it best suited her needs. Although the bank proposed naming the account "Mary A. Fraser, executrix of the estate of James R. Fraser," she said she wanted it to be opened as "The Estate of James R. Fraser." Free of charge, the bank ordered cheques printed for the account with the estate name above the signature line. This would clearly show that when Mary signed estate cheques, she would be signing as executrix and not in a personal capacity. Into the account Mary would deposit all the money she received for the estate, and all payments related to the estate would be made from it. In this way the account would provide a lasting record of all cash transactions Mary would make in her function as trustee for the estate.

When asked for a copy of the will appointing her executrix, Mary handed the bank her certified copy of probate which stated that the appointed executrix had full authority over all estate matters. The bank had no need to have a copy of the will because it had no responsibility for adjudicating the distribution of estate assets. To conserve Mary's supply of the documents, the bank's customer services officer made a photocopy and returned the original to her.

Mary then asked the bank to arrange a transfer of Jim's chequing account, redeem his $15,000 GIC with the Bank of Montreal, and have the money deposited to the new estate account. While Jim's GIC did not mature until November 6, 1996, it could be redeemed now without penalty, with interest paid to date, because of his death. (Financial institutions allow early redemption of otherwise non-redeemable GICs because the money may be urgently needed to pay funeral expenses and other obligations.) Mary was told

that the transaction would be completed in a couple of days, with no service charges. She signed the required transfer forms as executrix, and gave one of her certified copies of probate to be sent to the Bank of Montreal. Also, she arranged for the transfer of the Bank of Montreal savings account, a joint account in both their names, to her personal Scotiabank account. Because it was a joint account, with loss payable to survivor, it was not an estate asset. She also asked the Scotiabank staff if they could get the Bank of Montreal to return her passbook, for her records.

By 27 June Mary found she had enough money in the estate's bank account to pay accumulated bills, the two charitable donations, and the gifts to her grandchildren. Knowing that the $5,000 to each child was intended to help with their education, and that Jim would have liked it invested for that purpose, Mary wrote a letter to their mother Elizabeth so she would have a receipt (exhibit no. 13) for the payments. When she handed the cheques over she suggested to Elizabeth that, as interest rates were presently quite low, she consider putting the money into the shares of a well established company, like a major bank, which would provide a dividend reinvestment programme. Hopefully, by the time the children became eighteen years of age, the investments would have grown enough to help significantly in furthering their education. (If clause 9 of Jim's will had not provided that the bequests to the children be given to a parent, it may have been necessary for the estate to hold the $10,000 in trust until the children reached the age of majority, or else set up trust accounts for them with a financial institution.)

Mary decided it was time to empty the safety deposit box and see exactly what it contained. Only one key to the box had been found; with it and one of her copies of probate, staff at the Bank of Montreal let Mary have unrestricted access to the box. She emptied the contents into one of Jim's briefcases, terminated the lease, and learned that the lost key charge was equal to the rental refund. Mary took everything home and made the following list, headed "Bank of Montreal safety deposit box contents" :

• Canada Savings Bonds Series R46 5 @ $5,000 in name of James Fraser total $25,000;

• 1,000 shares Bank of Nova Scotia, common "James Fraser";

• 1,000 shares Nova Scotia Power, common "James Fraser";

• 500 shares Air Canada, common "James Fraser";

• Envelope containing variety of gold and other coins;

• Envelope containing old Canadian and United States stamps;

• $25,000 Maritime Life Insurance policy on Jim's life naming me beneficiary;

• $10,000 Canada Life Insurance policy on Jim's life naming me beneficiary;

• 100 shares Prenior Financial Ltd. common "James Fraser";

• 10,000 shares Memorah Mines Ltd. signed on the back by stockbroker Richardson Greenshields with a letter saying it was in "street form" (i.e., the same as a cheque payable to bearer);

• Insurance certificate issued by Commercial Travellers Association to James Fraser, loss payable to estate, death payment amount not stated.

A trip to the Bank of Montreal concerning Jim's RRSP account was all that was needed to transfer the funds entirely to a new RRSP in Mary's name without a charge. The only documentation required was a proof of death. The bank made a copy of one Mary had with her, and returned the original to her. Because Jim had died, the account could be transferred to his spouse without any income tax consequences, and it did not form part of his estate. The bank gave Mary some pamphlets describing their RRSP services.

Mary was at a loss as to what to do with Jim's stamp and coin collections because of the difficulties in establishing values for them. Stamps and coins do not trade on any established market like investments do; quality, scratches, post marks, and so on, affect their sale value, and pricing catalogues are just a guide for professionals, knowledgeable collectors and dealers. One option for Mary was to use catalogue information to divide the collections into four hopefully equal shares, and give one share to Elizabeth and one to Chris. She asked them if they wanted that done. Neither had any interest in the collections so Mary decided she would sell them for whatever she could get, and took the collections to three local coin and stamp dealers. They did not offer to buy the stamps, but were eager to purchase the coins. Mary received three offers for the coins, ranging from $1,500 to $2,500. She accepted the $2,500 offer and deposited the money in the estate bank account, along with cheques from Jim's company for everything it owed him, including a refund of Canada Savings Bond payroll deductions and vacation pay. She also deposited a $305 income tax refund for December 1995. She put the stamp collection in her own safety deposit box. Some time in the future, she thought, it might be of value, or perhaps the grandchildren might like it when they were older. But, the dealers had told her, the days when amateur stamp collections could be expected to be valuable had gone.

V

TRANSACTIONS AND VALUING ASSETS

mong Jim's papers Mary had found his 1996 renewal membership card and benefits letter from the Commercial Travellers' Association. She wrote to them, stating that James had died, and asked what they needed to pay his death benefit. Within a few days she received their letter enclosing a claim form to be completed and returned accompanied with a death certificate, certified copy of probate, and Jim's membership card or certificate. Mary filled out the claim form, found his membership card in his wallet, and mailed the requested documents to the Association's office. Within two weeks she received a cheque for $3,125, payable to Jim's estate.

Jim had taken out life insurance policies for $25,000 and $10,000 many years earlier, and they became payable on May 24, 1996, the day he died. It was not until June 27 that Mary contacted the companies to get their claims forms. She completed and returned the forms, along with two proofs of death and certified copies of probate. Three weeks later, cheques for $10,098.75 and $25,246.75 arrived, payable to Mary Fraser. While $35,000 of the money was tax-free, Mary would receive T5

slips for the $345.50 interest earned on this amount from May 24 until the day it was paid to her.

Mary had always liked driving Jim's 1995 Buick and was happy it had been left to her. She went to the Registry of Motor Vehicles office with certificates of registration for both cars and her Letters Testamentary to which was attached a copy of the will. The representative carefully examined the court document, and, satisfied that the will stated to whom the vehicles were to be transferred, prepared new vehicle ownership certificates. The cost of the certificate and new license plate for the Buick was $124, and $98 for Elizabeth's Honda. Mary wrote a cheque on the estate's account for $222 in payment. The representative explained that when ownership of a motor vehicle was changed to comply with the terms of a will or an estate, sales taxes were not applicable. Mary was told to immediately remove the old plates; if they were returned to the Registry, a cheque would be sent to the estate for whatever refunds were owing. That afternoon Elizabeth put the new plates on what was now her Honda and her mother's Buick and returned the old plates to the Motor Vehicles office.

The day before, Mary had phoned the Frasers' insurance agent to arrange policy cancellations on both cars and a new insurance policy on the Buick effective when she acquired ownership. Within a few days an insurance premium refund cheque, for $438.90 payable to the estate, arrived, along with a new policy on the Buick and a bill for Mary to pay. A week later the estate received a $96 refund cheque from the motor vehicles department.

To establish values for Jim's two cars, Mary asked at her bank what values they would use if taking them to secure loans. A letter from one of the loan officers told her that Red Book values in May for similarly equipped models were $17,600 for a 1995 Buick and $4,560 for a Honda Civic. These valuations were obtained so that they could be used for completing the appraisal of estate assets.

After looking through the last couple of Jim's monthly statements from Acadia Investments, Mary phoned George Anderson, who was listed on the form as the investment advisor. Surprised and sorry to hear of Jim's death, he asked if there was anything he could do to be of assistance. He added that while he could help with information, he could not act on any instructions until provided with a copy of probate or a similar document showing that she was the sole executrix. Some of Jim's securities were not held through Acadia Investments, but for the sake of convenience, she agreed to take all of them to Mr. Anderson. That put all Jim's investments, except his Canada Savings Bonds, in one place.

Anderson agreed to prepare a list of all securities James owned on May 24th with valuations using market prices the day before his death, as Revenue Canada requires all estate assets to be valued as at the day before death. (Stock market "high," "low," and "closing" prices are published daily in newspapers.) He explained that when valuing investment portfolios, market closing prices are used. However,

in the event there were no trades in a company's shares on the specific date, then any outstanding bid price for the shares is used. For Jim's investments, closing prices on May 23 were easily obtained.

Later that day Mary took a certified copy of probate and Jim's stock certificates to Acadia Investments' office. Anderson gave her a receipt for the securities and said that in order for his company to hold and deal with these shares it would be necessary to get them registered in the name of his company. To do this, she, as executrix, would have to sign forms known as a Declaration of Transmission (exhibit no. 14) and a Power of Attorney to Transfer Securities (exhibit no. 15) for each stock. These forms will be accepted by trust company stock transfer departments, who are agents for the companies whose share certificates are presently registered in James' name. Mr. Anderson said they would need at least one more copy of probate to use in dealing with the trust company stock transfer agents. He agreed to have the transmission and attorney forms ready for Mary's signature as executrix the next day. He also explained that his company had a resident commissioner of oaths who would witness her signatures on the declaration of transmission forms. This was a courtesy service to valued clients which the company was pleased to provide.

A few days later Mary received a letter listing all Jim's investments with valuations as at market close on May 23, 1996:

VALUATION OF CASH AND SECURITIES AT ACADIAN INVESMENTS INC.

- 2,000 shares Canadian Pacific,
  common @ $24.25 $48,500

- 2,000 shares Maritime Tel & Tel,
  common @ 21.00   42,000

- 500 shares NorTel,
  common @ 65.50   32,750
- Cash account   4,125

TOTAL   **$127,375**

VALUATION OF OTHER SECURITIES

- 500 shares Air Canada,
  common @ 4.25   2,125

- 1,000 shares Bank of Nova Scotia,
  common @ 32.50   32,500

- 10,000 shares Memorah Mines, name changed
  to Memora Resources Inc. @ 0.26   2,600

- 1,000 shares Nova Scotia Power,
  common @ 11.25   11,250

- 100 shares Prenior Trust, defunct, no value.

After dealing with Jim's investments, Mary next turned to the matter of the Chester Basin cottage, which had been the family's summer vacation home and the place of many happy times. Both Mary and James had never given any thought to selling it, so she had no idea what it was worth. The 1996 property tax assessment had been $43,000, the cottage and property were well maintained, and similar ocean front properties were seldom offered for sale. The property was certainly worth much more than its assessed value, but a reasonable market valuation as at May 23 had to be established. Since Jim's will passed ownership to Christopher there were income tax capital gains consequences to be considered. Mary decided to contact a real estate sales company, which she noticed had a few "For Sale" signs on properties in the Chester Basin area, for an opinion of how much it was worth. She explained

that she simply wanted a written opinion based on comparable sales data for the past year or so. She agreed to pay $100 for the service, and a week later the company's letter arrived containing sales information on several comparable properties. The letter concluded by stating the cottage would probably sell for $154,000, which, after commissions, would net $144,760 for the vendor.

This information prompted Mary to study the family household insurance policies. Basic insurance for the Crichton Avenue dwelling was $145,000 and for its contents $65,000; the Chester Basin cottage was covered for $92,000 and its contents $50,000. All policies carried a $500 deductible and would expire on April 15, 1997. The numbers seemed reasonable, but before putting the policies back in her files Mary phoned the agency to ask for an endorsement changing the policy for Crichton Avenue to be in her name only. Insurance on the Chester Basin cottage would be Christopher's responsibility when ownership was transferred to him.

When the home on Crichton Avenue had been purchased in 1959, title had been put in both James' and Mary's names as joint tenants. Mary now phoned the Registry of Deeds for Halifax County and asked them what documents were needed to change ownership of the home to her name alone. Somewhat to her surprise, they told her they would simply change their records. Anyone doing a title search of the property would easily find documents registered in Halifax County proving that she was the surviving joint tenant and owner.

Mary paid estate bills as they arrived. She had recovered from the estate account the $1,050 fee paid to the registrar of probate to open the estate and the $32.10 she had paid on behalf of the estate for the *Royal Gazette* advertisement. She wrote on all invoices the dates they had been paid and the cheque numbers used to pay them, and placed the vouchers in the "Disbursements" folder. When

Jim's final Mastercard bill arrived, Mary paid the $697.60 owing and noted he had accumulated 17,759 air miles. She had previously written to Mastercard, Canadian Tire, and Diners Club to cancel Jim's cards. Now she wrote to the issuer, the Bank of Montreal, asking whether Jim's balance was life insured, and requesting them to transfer the accumulated miles to her name. (Mary was aware that insurance coverage was provided on some credit cards; if James's Mastercard provided life insurance covering whatever was owing, the insurance would repay the amount.) The bank asked for a copy of the will and told her that amounts owing on the account were not life insured. Mary sent them a Letters Testamentary which had a copy of the will attached. A month later the bank informed Mary half the miles had been transferred to her, 25 per cent to Elizabeth, and 25 per cent to Christopher in accordance with the terms of the will. While these items actually could be considered estate disbursements, a monetary value for them was not given by the bank. Since the air miles had little if any sale value, Mary decided not to record them in the estate's inventory. She considered them to be a non-monetary item similar to Jim's suits, golf clubs, rifle,* sports books, workshop tools, gold watch, and so on, which had already been given to Elizabeth and Christopher. To try to put dollar values on such items would just increase probate fees, and probate courts are inclined not to expect such items to be listed in inventories. The three Frasers as residual heirs were the only people with an interest in the distribution of such personal items and had amicably agreed on how they would be divided. In any event, the will gave Mary the authority to value, in her uncontrolled discretion, any estate assets.

A week after the funeral Mary had received a

*Before he took the gun Christopher had called the police department to find out about registration regulations and what he had to do to comply with them.

couple of pamphlets from City Funeral Home, published by cemetery monument companies, and put them in her "Monument for cemetery" file. Now that she had the time to think about getting a monument, Mary dug out the pamphlets and phoned both companies asking for suggestions and prices. She wanted a stone to be placed in Sackville Cemetery for under $2000 if possible. One company sent a letter with glossy pictures of different kinds of stone with varying prices. They invited her to visit their office to see the displays. The other company's representative phoned to say it would be better for them to meet Mary at the cemetery to get an idea of what she and her family would like. This sounded like a good idea to her.

They met at the cemetery as planned, looking at the various monuments and lettering styles as they strolled toward Jim's grave. Mary liked the look and shape of some more than others, and gradually her choices began to narrow. Eventually she found the type and size of stone she liked and decided to have the family name FRASER inscribed at the top in simple, easy-to-read lettering. Jim's name and dates would be on the face below. In recognition of the fact that Mary might as some point remarry, the consultant suggested that sufficient space be left for her name to be added when she died, but not put on the stone at this time. While Mary did not feel quite comfortable with the idea, it seemed to make sense to her so she agreed. The consultant explained the differences between sawn and polished stone on the top and sides, and the advantages of curved versus square tops, and pointed out where ice and rain had damaged some of the stones. She also told her that winter freezing could cause monuments to shift, and a bevelled base would help avoid the problem. Mary noticed that many memorial stones did not have any name on the back and she decided she wanted FRASER there too. After they had come to a tentative agreement on the look of the memorial stone, the company representative told Mary she would send a computerized sketch of it for Mary to confirm the details. With the sketch would be a listing of prices, including installation. During their meeting the consultant had directed Mary's attention to a number of memorials her company had provided in the $2,000 price range.

When the computerized sketch arrived, Mary examined it carefully. It had a space for another name to be added, but the lettering was arranged so that it would not look unbalanced without it. Jim's date of birth was not correct, so she changed it. The price, including tax, to be paid by the estate, was $2,139.00. Before phoning the monument company's consultant Mary asked Elizabeth and Chris to drop in to see the sketch. Both agreed it looked fine and thanked her for asking for their input.

A few days later a corrected monument sketch arrived, together with a purchase order for Mary to sign and return. She checked it and the sketch carefully, knowing that once she signed and returned the purchase agreement the estate would be responsible for the costs of correcting any errors she had made in the specifications and wording. She signed, approving the sketch and also the purchase order, kept copies for her records, and returned the papers to the company. Two months later she got a phone call from the company representative, saying the monument had been installed. Mary went to inspect it and it met with her approval, so she told Chris and Elizabeth that their father's memorial was in place.

Mary had set up a simple bookkeeping system the same day she had opened the estate's bank account. She had taken two blank sheets of paper and headed one RECEIPTS—MONEY RECEIVED (exhibit no. 16A) and the other page DISBURSEMENTS—EXPENSES (exhibit no. 16B). The first page was to be used to record information about all money received by the estate: amount, date, and cumulative total. The second page was to be used to record when money is paid out by the estate, cheque number, to whom paid, why, the amount and a cumulative total of payments. The difference between receipts and disbursements would equal the balance in the bank account. By the time the estate was settled the two pages would make a complete record of all monetary transactions involving it. It would not, of course, record the transfer of ownership of the two cars and cottage as no money had changed hands in these instances.

Near the end of July, Mary made another visit to the office of lawyer Richard Clarke. She wanted him to prepare a deed transferring ownership of the Chester Basin cottage to Christopher. Before her visit, he asked her if she had a copy of the present deed, because this would save the nuisance and expense of getting a copy from the registry office. She removed the deed and the latest tax bill from her files and took them to Clarke's office. A few days later, his office phoned to say that the warranty deed was ready for her signature. When Mary came to sign the deed, Clarke said that he had not had a title search done but understood there were no encumbrances on the property. She confirmed that its taxes and mortgage had been paid, and added that she had found a letter among Jim's papers stating that title had been searched when he had bought it. He told her he would send the deed to Bridgewater, where the Registry of Deeds for Lunenburg County is located.

While she was signing the deed Clarke asked if she and Christopher had signed any agreement regarding her continued unrestricted use of the cottage. If they had not, he suggested, they should do so, because the future is unpredictable and relationships sometimes change. She and Chris, she told him, had briefly discussed the desirability of having some sort of agreement, but had not made any formal arrangement. Mary asked Mr. Clarke to prepare a simple agreement for them to sign. He agreed to have one ready for signing the following

Thursday and recommended she and Chris both review it and make revisions if necessary.

After Mary and Chris discussed the document Mr. Clarke had prepared and made a few revisions, they signed the agreement (exhibit no. 17) in triplicate in Clarke's office. All three of them kept a copy. Christopher made a notation on his copy that, for future income tax, capital gain, or loss calculation purposes, his deemed acquisition cost of the property was $144,750.

At the beginning of August, Acadia Investments sent Mary a summary of the transactions in James's account from January 1 to July 31, 1996:

- Cash account balance as of December 31, 1995: $2,367.88
- Dividend income January 1 to May 24, 1996:
- January 15, 2,000 shares Maritime Tel & Tel, common: 640.00
- January 28, 2,000 shares Canadian Pacific, common: 240.00
- March 30, 500 shares Northern Telecom Communications (NorTel), common: 65.00
- April 15, 2,000 shares Maritime Tel & Tel, common: 640.00
- April 28, 2,000 shares Canadian Pacific, common: 240.00
- Interest paid January 1 to May 24: 21.30
- Cash account balance as of May 24: 4,214.18
- June 30, 500 shares NorTel Communications, common: 65.00
- July 15, 2,000 shares Maritime Tel & Tel, common: 640.00
- July 28, 2,000 shares Canadian Pacific, common: 240.00
- Total interest paid May 31, June 30, and July 31: 13.98
- Total cash balance in the account as of July 31, 1996: 5,173.16

Mary asked Mr. Anderson, the investment adviser, to send all the accounts' cash balances to her with the monthly statements. This would make it easier for her to keep track of the dividend and interest earnings for each month and keep all the estate money in one place. He told her that although Jim had been in the habit of letting the cash account build up until he either bought an investment or asked for a cheque, the instructions on the account would be changed to suit Mary's needs, and money sent as requested.

By now Mary felt clearly in control of all the estate's assets and was ready to prepare a detailed inventory for presentation to the registrar of probate. While the three-month deadline to file the Warrant of Appraisement of Inventory did not expire until September 20, it was now near the end of August and her two appraisers had told her they were ready whenever she was. Mary prepared and typed a list of Jim's assets, with real estate recorded under the usual legal name of "Real Property," and everything else under "Personal Property."

ESTATE OF JAMES ROBERT FRASER
INVENTORY VALUATIONS MAY 24, 1996

REAL PROPERTY
Cottage
  At Chester Basin, Lunenburg Co. $144,760.00

REAL PROPERTY VALUATION TOTAL   **$144,760.00**

PERSONAL PROPERTY
Bank Accounts and Cash
  Bank of Montreal, checking account: 3,675.25
  Bank of Montreal, GIC, 6.5%, due July 4, 1996: 15,000.00
  Interest accrued to May 24th on GIC: 867.75
  Coin collection: 2,500.00
  Account at Acadia Investments Inc.: 4,214.18
  TOTAL 26,257.18

Investments

2,000 shs Canadian Pacific, common:	48,500.00
2,000 shs Maritime Tel & Tel, common:	42,000.00
500 shs NorTel, common:	32,750.00
500 shs Air Canada, common:	2,125.00
1,000 shs Bank of Nova Scotia:	32,500.00
10,000 shs Memora Resources Inc.:	2,600.00
1,000 shs Nova Scotia Power, common:	11,250.00
$25,000 Canada Savings Bonds, Series R46:	25,000.00
Interest accrued to May 1 on Canada Savings Bonds:	843.75
TOTAL	197,568.75

Vehicles

1995 Buick Century:	17,600.00
1991 Honda Civic:	4,560.00
TOTAL	22,160.00

Accounts Receivable

Final salary payment:	1,765.13
1995 income tax refund:	305.00
Refund CSB purchase payments:	875.00
Car insurance refunds:	438.90
Car license refunds:	96.00
Canada Pension death benefit:	3,540.00
TOTAL	7,020.03

Life Insurance

Commercial Travellers Association:	3,125.00

PERSONAL PROPERTY VALUATION TOTAL $256,130.96

Feeling quite confident her information was correct and neatly prepared, Mary was now ready to have the two appraisers check it. There was just one more thing to do with the information: summarize it on the inventory valuation document. This was attached to the Warrant of Appraisement she had received from the registrar of probate in June when the will was probated. She listed the value of the real estate at Chester Basin as $144,760 at the top of the document under the heading Real Property, and below it, under the heading Personal Property, the five groups of other assets, totalling $256,131. (Nova Scotia probate courts base their fee on the value of the deceased person's personal property and not on his or her real estate because title to the latter frequently just passes to the family; valuations may be relatively large and real estate generally requires little administrative work by the executor. If the real estate is subsequently sold, proceeds are included in the final accounting report made to the heirs and to probate court.) Mary could now arrange a meeting with Mr. Belliveau, the bank manager, and Christopher's accountant friend, Peter Wilford. After several phone calls, it was agreed that all three of them would meet the following morning at 10:45 A.M. in Mr. Belliveau's office.

In her briefcase, Mary had the letter from Valuation Real Estate Limited stating their opinion that $144,760 was a reasonable value for the Chester Basin cottage; the note from the bank with its valuation of the two cars; and Acadia Investments' letter giving the values of Jim's stocks. She also had the estate's cheque book and bank statements. After introductions, Wilford and Belliveau carefully examined the estate inventory Mary had prepared. As appraisers, they were responsible for judging the value of the estate's assets shown to them, to the best of their ability and knowledge. Mary handed them the valuation letters and told them about selling the coin collection after getting three bids for it. She had been unable to get bids for Jim's stamp collection, which, being of no value did not have to go on the inventory. The two appraisers checked her additions, agreed with the numbers and complimented her on having the information well organized and easy for them to check and verify. The next step was to get the probate court's appraisal documents attested by both appraisers. They had to meet with Mary and her lawyer to do this, so while they were still at the bank, she phoned Richard Clarke's office for an appointment.

When the time for the appointment came, Mary, Louis Belliveau and Peter Wilford arrived at Clarke's office. The lawyer examined the Appraisement of Inventory and accompanying valuation page with details. He then asked Belliveau and Wilford if they would swear that the facts therein were true. Both agreed and signed the Warrant of Appraisement (exhibit no. 10A) and the Appraisement of Inventory (exhibit no.18). Mary had to sign only the latter. After Clarke signed as a barrister of the Supreme Court of Nova Scotia, the documents were complete. At Mary's request, he had photocopies made of these completed documents for her records. The originals would be retained by the registrar of probate when she took them to the registrar's office.

Mary and the two appraisers then left the lawyer's office; she thanked them for their assistance and asked what she owed for their services. Both said they were glad to have been able to do something for her, since she was Jim's widow, and they did not expect to be paid. Back home, Mary wrote them thank-you notes, enclosing $75 cheques and suggesting they take themselves out to dinner. After all, as appraisers they had assumed legal responsibilities under oath and a simple thank-you did not seem adequate.

Mary then wrote a letter to the registrar of probate (exhibit no. 19) which she then delivered with the completed inventory valuation documents. When the letter and documents were handed to the probate office, one of the staff calculated the additional fee to be paid based on the higher actual value of the personal property of the estate.

It had been estimated at $236,000 when probate was granted on June 20 which made the opening fee $980 plus a charge for extra copies. The additional cost, based on a final valuation of $256,131, was only $105, which Mary paid with a cheque drawn on the estate's account.

KEEPING IN TOUCH

Mary arranged an evening dinner with Christopher, Elizabeth and her husband, and their two children. After dinner Mary gave her daughter and son an update on estate matters. Jim's final income tax return had to be prepared and sent to Revenue Canada. Once the tax was paid, she explained, she would consider distributing some of Jim's assets. This could be done with cash or some of the investments, or a combination of both. It would be a bit more complicated, of course, to distribute the investments than to sell them and just distribute cash. Both Elizabeth and Christopher said that because of the mortgages on their homes they would prefer to get cash. Mary was under no legal requirement to seek her children's opinion on how to go about winding up the estate, but she understood their desires and decided to convert all the estate items to cash and make partial distributions, leaving ample money to pay taxes and any other costs. She would need help, she said, with the income tax returns, and Chris suggested she go to his accountant friend, Peter Wilford.

Wilford said he would be pleased to prepare the income tax returns required by Revenue Canada.

He explained that a final return would have to be filed reporting James's 1996 income from January 1 to his death on May 24. In James's case the return would not need to be sent in until the following April 30th.* Wilford said that unless Mary had some reason to delay being able to settle the estate, the final return should now be prepared and filed. She agreed to do so. He then asked her to gather the information needed to prepare the return, starting with a letter from James's employer giving the amounts they would report to Revenue Canada for him as taxable income for 1996, and the amounts deducted from his pay for Employment Insurance, the Canada Pension Plan, medical insurance, pension contributions, income tax, and so on. In addition to Jim's income information, Wilford wanted details of all estate expenses, interest, dividends, and money received and deposited in the bank account. Also, he wanted a copy of the estate's May 24 inventory and copies of James's tax returns for 1994 and 1995, including Revenue Canada's assessment notices and any

---

*Revenue Canada has an information pamphlet entitled "Preparing Returns for Deceased Persons," which explains the options for filing returns.

correspondence found with the returns. If these returns could not be located, he said, he would prepare a letter to Revenue Canada authorizing it to give him the information he needed, and have Mary sign the letter as executrix.

It was a few days before the postman delivered the phone company's letter containing Jim's payroll information. Mary tucked it inside Jim's old briefcase, along with the tax returns she needed, a copy of the May 24 inventory that Belliveau and Wilford had appraised, and her record of estate money received and paid out (exhibit nos. 16A and 16B). Wilford made a photocopy of Mary's receipts and expenditure pages, then gave them back to her. "It is important that you keep these records up-to-date, as we will need them when we do the estate's tax return," he told her. After quickly scanning the various papers, Wilford said it appeared there would be some taxable capital gains, and he would need help to establish the costs of James's investments. Mary agreed to authorize George Anderson at Acadia Investments to give Wilford any information he wanted about her husband's account.

It took Mr. Anderson nearly a week to get purchase dates and cost information for each of the stocks in James's portfolio. No cost records could be found for the stocks in the safety deposit box. Mary did not know when or where he had bought them, nor what he had paid. However, Anderson was able to establish when the certificates had been registered in James's name. He therefore used stock market closing prices on those dates, and added what his company's brokerage charges would have been at that time to come up with the "cost" numbers he needed to calculate capital gains or losses.

One bright spot was found when Wilford looked at James's tax return for 1994. In that year James had used the capital loss on his shares in Prenior

Trust and had taken advantage of the expiring capital gains exemption by deeming the Chester Basin cottage property's value to be $120,000 for tax purposes. With it valued at $144,760, the deemed taxable capital gain would be only $24,760. (Revenue Canada's tax rules would deem the cottage to have been disposed of the day before James died, the same as his stock investments.) Christopher would receive ownership of the cottage at a deemed value of $144,760. When he eventually disposed of the property, his taxable capital gain or loss would be calculated using that aquisition cost figure.

It took Wilford a bit longer than expected to complete James's May 24, 1996 final income tax return (exhibit no. 20, pages 1 and 4 only). Taxable capital gains, including $24,760 on the cottage were over $67,000. Of this, $50,000 was added to his income, which resulted in a total of $26,259 tax to be paid. The amount was larger than Mary had expected, and while payment could be delayed until the following April, she had decided with Elizabeth and Chris to sell the investments and pay the tax now. She felt even more certain of her decision when Wilford explained that Revenue Canada would not issue a tax clearance for James until his 1996 income tax return had been assessed and all taxes he owed had been paid. Furthermore, it was now the first of October, both Elizabeth and Christopher were looking forward to receiving their inheritances, and the estate could not be formally finalized without Revenue Canada's clearance certificate.

When Mary phoned Mr. Anderson to tell him to sell all the investments, he happily told her that the market had gone up quite a bit since May. While stock markets prices are not absolutely predictable, he said, so far prices, (in general,) would probably continue to rise for a while. Anderson suggested she delay selling just now.

While his advice might have merit, she thought, as far as the estate was concerned, money was needed now to pay income tax and be distributed to the beneficiaries. Furthermore, there was no guarantee stock prices would not go down. Mary decided that Anderson should sell everything over the next week or two, using his best judgement on timing. "Please try to have sales completed by October 11," she said.

Anderson sold all the shares and on the 15th delivered a cheque for $205,745.00, along with his listing of sale prices and proceeds (see below).

Mary promptly took the cheque to the bank, then wrote a cheque to Revenue Canada for $26,259.11, leaving $193,941.95 in the account. Wilford had told her that the income received by the estate and the capital gains realized by selling the investments for more than their May 24 value placed the estate in a taxable position. The estate's income tax liability could be passed on to Mary and the children, but if she planned for the estate to pay it, he said, the amount should be less than $10,000.

Mary decided she could now safely pay out $180,000 in partial distributions: $45,000 each to Elizabeth and Christopher, and $90,000 to herself. That would leave nearly $14,000 in the estate account, plus $25,000 in Canada Savings Bonds not yet cashed, which should be much more than enough to pay income taxes, closing costs, and any other estate expenses. Now that Jim's final income tax return had been completed and his tax paid, she felt that there was very little risk that any new claims could be made on the estate.

Richard Clarke had told Mary to keep receipts for all payments, including payments to herself, because the estate is a separate entity and as the executrix she was just the administrator and trustee appointed for it. While it seemed a bit too formal to document distribution payments to the children and to herself, Mary nonetheless prepared distribution receipt letters (exhibits no. 21 A, B and, C), in duplicate, to have signed copies for receipts. When the letters and cheques were completed she asked Elizabeth and Chris to drop in to pick theirs up and sign the receipt letters.

INVESTMENT	SALE PRICE	AMOUNT	COMMISSION	PROCEEDS
500 shares Air Canada, common	$4.90	2,450.00	80.00	2,370.00
2,000 shares Canadian Pacific, common	32.40	64,800.00	750.00	64,050.00
2,000 shares Maritime Tel & Tel, common	22.20	44,400.00	750.00	43,650.00
500 shares Nortel, common	83.20	41,600.00	325.00	41,275.00
1,000 shares Bank of Nova Scotia, common	40.15	40,150.00	400.00	39,750.00
10,000 shares Memora Resources	.15	1,500.00	175.00	1,325.00
1,000 shares Nova Scotia Power, common	13.60	13,600.00	275.00	13,325.00
TOTALS		$208,500.00	$2,755.00	$205,745.00

Note: Bank of Nova Scotia shares were sold X dividend; their October 26 dividend will be sent to you when received.˙

(X dividend indicates that shares were sold after the company had declared the dividend, but before it was paid. The purchaser knows the former owner will receive the dividend.)

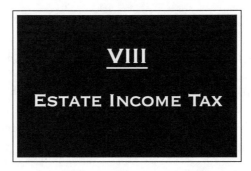

VIII

ESTATE INCOME TAX

During her meetings with Peter Wilford, Mary learned that it would probably take Revenue Canada about three months to complete its assessment of James's final income tax return. When it was finished, a notice of assessment would be sent stating the amount of additional tax, if any, that would have to be paid. As soon as the income taxes were paid in full, Mary could request that Revenue Canada issue a tax clearance certificate. This would relieve her, as the executrix, from personal liability for any unpaid taxes that might subsequently be discovered after the estate was closed. She also learned that the registrar of probate would require her to have a tax clearance certificate when she applied for a date to formally close the estate. Judging from the advice she had received, Mary thought it best to have a formal closing. A formal closing is not always required, but unless it takes place, the possibility exists that the executor could be held personally accountable for any previously unknown estate liabilities. The cost of a formal closing is not very high so Mary planned to have one as the best way to complete her executorship duties.

Wilford and Mary also discussed when to file the estate's first income tax return. As James had died between January 1 and October 31, 1996, the deadline for filing it and paying income tax would be April 30 of the following year. However, the most practical reporting date would be the same as for individuals: December 31. They agreed to have the estate's tax return prepared for the December date. Mary would take all the income tax-related documents, such as T4 and T5 slips she received for both James and the estate, to Wilford for him to use to prepare the return. She would also have to give him her updated list of money received for the estate (exhibit no. 16A).

With no more work to complete for the estate at the moment, Mary agreed to accompany her neighbour Ruby on a Caribbean cruise in January. Ruby's second husband was quite happy to stay home and keep an eye on Mary's house. Mary came back from her trip on January 21, tanned and ready to make a new life for herself.

As she went through the mail that had piled up in her absense, Mary found a letter from Revenue Canada enclosing the notice of assessment for Jim's May 24, 1996 tax return. Fortunately, the notice showed a zero balance. Mary could now apply for the tax clearance certificate. She picked up two copies of the required form from the local Revenue Canada office. It looked easy to complete but required that a copy of the will and all probate documents be attached. Mary made a photocopy of her Letters Testamentary with copy of will attached (exhibit no. 9). Then she completed the Request for Clearance Certificate (exhibit no. 22). The tax clearance form also asked for a statement of the deceased's assets and distribution plan. Mary included a copy of the May 24 inventory, which had been attached to the Appraisement of Inventory. She mailed all the forms together with a letter (exhibit no. 23) to Revenue Canada stating which assets had already been distributed, and what would be done with the remainder.

Mary filed the T4 and T5 slips, some in Jim's name and some in the estate's, in an envelope as they arrived. On March 1, she took them, her updated list of all money received by the estate, and the details of the investment sales to Wilford. He was overloaded with income tax work for other clients, so he introduced Mary to Beverly, his assistant, whom he had briefed on the Fraser file. Beverly took Mary's papers and explained that the estate had two options: it could pay tax on some or all of the taxable income it had earned since May 24, or the income could be allocated to the three beneficiaries. If the interest, dividends, and capital gains were allocated to Mary, Elizabeth, and Christopher, they would have to include the amounts as income when filing their December 31, 1996 tax returns.

In the end, either the estate would pay the income tax or its heirs would. Mary preferred not to place herself and her children in the position of having to pay income tax on money received from Jim's estate. Beverly asked a few more questions and said she would give Mary a call as soon as the return was ready.

Beverly phoned Mary on March 5 to say that the estate's December 31 tax return was completed and ready to be picked up. When Mary came by to get it Beverly explained to her what made up the $27,133.66 in taxable income and how $7,257.33 was calculated from this as the amount of income tax the estate would have to pay. Mary took home two copies of the T3 trust income tax and information return (exhibit no. 24 pages 1 and 4 only), wrote a cheque to the Receiver General, and mailed the original, keeping a copy for her files.

There was nothing more Mary could do but wait for Revenue Canada's Clearance Certificate (exhibit no. 25) to arrive. It came on May 19 and was dated "97-05-14." Now it was possible for her to complete her executrix responsibilities and proceed with the closing of the estate. The next thing she needed was an appointment with the registrar of probate for a closing date. When she phoned for the appointment she was asked whether she had received a tax clearance. She answered that she had, and the closing was then set for July 15 at 10.00 A.M. in the Court of Probate.

Mary did not understand why the closing date was nearly two months away until her lawyer Richard Clarke explained the various things that had to be done before that date. First, Mary would have to petition the registrar for a citation to close the estate, which would confirm the appointment. Second, the date and time of closing would have to be advertised for five weeks. Third, the registrar would require before the closing date, the estate's accounting report, which recorded what had been done with its May 24 inventory. Clarke asked how many people still had an interest in the estate as

creditors and residual beneficiaries. Mary answered that since all debts and bills had been paid, the balance of the estate was left to her two children and herself. She added that the income taxes had been paid and that she had received a tax clearance certificate. He undertook to gather together the documents required by the registrar to legally confirm the closing date, and have them ready for her to sign the following afternoon.

The Petition to Close (exhibit no. 26A and 26B) was a two-part document. The first part related basic facts about the estate and requested an appointment on Mary's behalf for her to present the estate's accounting report to the court for audit and approval. Attached to it was a photocopy of the ad she had placed in the *Royal Gazette's* June 26, 1966 issue. The petition required only Mary's signature. The second part was an affidavit wherein she swore that the facts stated in the first document were true. She signed this and Clarke signed and put his seal on it. He also provided unsigned duplicates marked "COPY" for her files.

In addition to the petition, Mary received four copies of a document identified as a Citation to Close (exhibit no. 28). Clarke said they were for the registrar to sign, keeping one copy and returning to Mary three signed copies, one to be given to each residual beneficiary.

Wednesday morning Mary took her covering letter (exhibit no. 27) and the documents to the registrar's office. She was told that the Citation to Close would be ready in the afternoon when the registrar would have signed and sealed them. There was no charge.

She had been told by Clarke that when she received the registrar's Citation to Close, she would have to have a notice published in the *Royal Gazette*. Mary wrote a letter to the publisher (exhibit no. 29) and took it and one of the copies of her citation to their office. They made a copy of the citation for themselves and told her that the notice would be published in the following five issues. A copy of the June 4 issue of the *Gazette* (exhibit no. 30) arrived a week later, containing the notice.

Mary still had to get a final account made of the estate's assets, receipts, and disbursements. This account or summary is the integral part of the closing documents, which also include the executor's affidavit and the final decree for the registrar to sign. She would need to give copies of it and of the Citation to Close to Elizabeth and Chris, as residual beneficiaries, and prove that she had done so. She could have them sign receipts if the items were hand-delivered, or she could use registered mail. Clarke had said he would prepare the final set of documents needed to formally close the estate as soon as he had received Wilford's accounting summary. The package would have to be in the registrar's office at least ten days before the July 15 closing.

Peter Wilford was experienced in preparing estate accounting reports for court presentations in the format Mary needed. She gave him her list of receipts and expenditures. Two days later Wilford's office phoned to say the final account of Mary Ann Fraser (exhibit No. 31) was ready to be picked up. When she stopped in to get it he explained that although he did not presently know the amount of bank interest earned by the estate for June and July, the amounts would be too small to be of any consequence to the registrar in approving the account. He pointed out that he had set up a $500 reserve which should cover his and the lawyer's fees.

To fulfil the requirement that beneficiaries and others with an interest in the estate be formally notified of the date, time, and place of a closing, Mary followed the usual practice of sending registered letters. She sent photocopies of Wilford's accounting summary and of the Citation to Close with her letter of notification of closing (exhibit no. 32) to both Elizabeth and Christopher by registered mail on June 5. This gave them more than 30 days' notice of the closing date, which was more than ample time for them to examine and question her accounts.

A copy of the executor's final account must be provided to the registrar at least ten days before the closing date to leave sufficient time for it to be checked for accuracy, and to determine that bequests and distributions have been made in accordance with the terms of the will. Mary gave Clarke's office a copy of Wilford's accounting report, the names and addresses of the other two residual beneficiaries, and two postal receipts for the registered letters she had sent to Elizabeth and Christopher. The next day she was asked for the date that the notice of closing had first been published in the *Royal Gazette*. She pulled her issue of the *Gazette* from her documents folder and told the lawyer's office it was June 4, 1997.

Mary was given a June 19 appointment to receive and sign the final documents at Richard Clarke's office. There he presented the three documents needed for the closing. The first one was a statement which she signed under oath, called the Executor's Affidavit (exhibit no. 33). It had two attachments: a photocopy of the page from the *Royal Gazette's* June 4, 1997 issue (exhibit no. 30) advertising the date, time and place of the closing; and a page to which Mary's registered mail postal receipts were attached to prove that Citation to Close notices had been sent to Elizabeth and Christopher. If she had not used registered mail, it would have been necessary to attach some other evidence that these notices had been given to them.

The second document was the executor's Final Account (exhibit no. 34), the affidavit to which Peter Wilford's accounting report (exhibit no. 31) was attached. At the formal closing, the registrar would examine Mary's account of the administration of the estate. When the registrar was fully satisfied with Mary's responses, she would ask her to swear that the information and accounts were correct. Then the amount of the court's fee for the session would be added to estate disbursements under CLOSING EXPENSES. (This fee is set according to the scale for probate fees in the Province.) When Wilford had prepared Mary's accounting report, he had calculated it based on the "value administered by executor" recorded as $292,871.77 on page 1 of Mary's account (exhibit no. 31). He put $632 on the summary page, knowing that if the registrar did not agree, she would change it.

Registrars have the authority to fix the amount of commission or fee executors may receive over and above such necessary expenses as they see just and reasonable. The maximum fee in Nova Scotia is five per cent calculated on the value of the estate. (Unsold real property is not included in the amount received.) Percentage rates vary depending on the size of the estate, the amount of time and responsibility involved in its execution, the ages and marital status of the deceased's family, and so on. Mary had not bothered to recover out-of-pocket expenses incurred by her on behalf of the estate because they had not amounted to very much, and because she expected that any charges she made to the estate might be closely questioned.

Having given consideration to the matter of requesting an executrix fee, she had decided not to do so because it would represent taxable income. Mary would receive fifty per cent of the residue of the estate tax-free (taxes were paid already by the estate), so, she thought, why should she take a fee and indirectly donate some of Jim's money to the government by paying income tax on the fee? Also, in view of the fact that the estate had not been a complicated one to administer, the registrar might not allow a full five percent fee. Even if she did, Mary reasoned, income tax would take thirty-five to forty percent of it from her.

The third document, the Final Decree (exhibit no. 35), was to be signed and sealed by the registrar to formally settle the estate and terminate the court's involvement with it. It would then become an order of the court and Mary would be asked to pay the court's fee for the closing and would be given a copy of the decree for her records. Copies of the three documents had been made for Mary's files.

As soon as the court's fee and the amounts owing to Richard Clarke and Peter Wilford had been paid, Mary would be able to distribute what was left in the bank account to her children and herself. Wilford had advised her that the estate's final income tax return simply allocated any taxable income earned from January 1, 1997, until final distribution, to the three beneficiaries. He told Mary that it would be a good idea to make a photocopy of the decree and put the original in her safety deposit box.

Mary wrote a letter to the registrar (exhibit no. 36) to have a record of the date she delivered the documents. The deadline for sending them to the registrar was ten days before the closing date and she was well ahead of that. Since she had been asked if she had a tax clearance certificate, it seemed like a good idea to attach a copy of it to her letter.

When Mary looked over the documents it seemed certain to her that the registrar would be satisfied both with Mary's accounting report and her administration of the estate's assets as directed by the will. From her files Mary selected folders containing the estate bank statements, disbursement receipts, investment sales reports, and her list of money received and spent. For easy reference, she sorted the paid invoices, bills, and receipts and put them in the same order as the corresponding cheque numbers. She put the folders and a copy of her June 27 letter to the registrar with its attachments in her briefcase, ready for July 15.

The evening before the closing Mary took a last look through her files. Everything was in order. She knew all there was to know about the estate because she had done it all.

Mary had hoped that both her children would be able to go to court for the closing, but, Christopher would not be able to make it. He told her, however, that he did not have any unanswered questions concerning the estate.

Promptly at 10.00 A.M. Mary and Elizabeth were ushered into the room used for the Court of Probate. The registrar, Susan Cole, introduced herself and Mary introduced her daughter. No one else was present. Proceedings began with Mary placing her hand on a Bible to swear that she would tell the truth. The registrar asked for evidence of the ownership transfer of the Chester Basin cottage to Christopher Fraser. Mary exhibited lawyer Richard Clarke's bill for $342.67 which stated that the property had been deeded to Christopher.

"Have all debts and liabilities been settled?" the registrar asked.

"Yes, except two small bills for accounting and legal work," Mary replied. "A reserve for $500 has been set up, which is sufficient to cover them."

In fact, both Wilford and Clarke had already been paid. Mary also had recovered the $7.15 she had paid to send registered letters to the other two residual beneficiaries, the total of these three payments was less than $500.

The registrar commented that even though interest rates had been low some interest income had been obtained, which was good. She went on to mention the importance that executors manage the funds under their control for the benefit of the beneficiaries. "Sometimes I see estates where substantial amounts of money have been held and no effort made to earn interest," she said. "That's not satisfactory administration!" She complimented Mary on doing a good job and asked what commission she felt she should receive. Mary replied that, as she was a residual beneficiary, she did not want a fee.

Peter Wilford's calculation of $632.00 as the court's fee proved to be correct. After it was deducted, the balance left for distribution was $32,417.41. This was recorded near the bottom of the final account summary (exhibit no. 31 page 1). Mary wrote an estate cheque to pay the court fee. The registrar signed and sealed the final decree and handed it to Mary. Court then adjourned.

All that was left for Mary to do now was to have Peter Wilford prepare a final tax return for the estate, pay his bill, and give the remainder to Elizabeth, Chris, and herself.

When Mary received her July bank statement she phoned Peter Wilford and told him how much interest had been earned by the estate in June and July. This amount, $83.51, was the only information he needed to complete the estate's final income tax return. He charged $157.50 for this. Because he allocated the small amount of interest income earned in 1997 to the three residual beneficiaries, no tax had to be paid by the estate.

After Wilford was paid there was $32,349.77 left in the bank account. Mary wrote a cheque for half to herself, divided the rest between Elizabeth and Christopher, and closed the bank account.

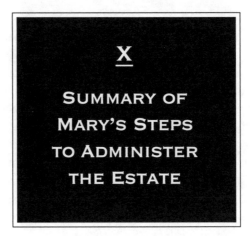

Upon reflection Mary was pleased with what she had done. She had settled Jim's estate in a manner she knew would have pleased him; he liked to see people take on unfamiliar tasks and see them through. Mary had done it all in less than fifteen months and in so doing had learned a lot about the process. It had not been an arduous job, but rather an interesting one. She had met new people. The registrar and her staff had been friendly, helpful, and considerate. Mary now knew more about investments, accounting services, and how and when to use lawyers. She was glad Jim had kept family business within the family by appointing her his executor rather than asking a business associate, lawyer, or trust company. She had delayed changing her own will much longer than she should have, but she wanted to wait until she knew what the whole executorship process was.

"Now would be a good time to tell Elizabeth and Chris what an executor has to do, how he or she must do it, how to keep costs down and where to go for help when needed," Mary said to herself. "Perhaps it will be easiest if I list the steps I took

in detail, mentioning the special documents I needed and the process followed."

Mary's list looked like this:

1. ***Made funeral arrangements*** [exhibit no. 1];

2. ***Got six proof of death certificates from the funeral home;***

3. ***Found Jim's last will*** [exhibit No. 2];

4. ***Had a lawyer prepare court documents to have the will probated and myself appointed executrix.*** The documents prepared for me were:

4.1 ***Oath of Executor*** [exhibit no. 3] ***swearing that the will was the last one James had made;***

4.2 ***Petition to Grant Probate*** [exhibit nos. 4A and 4B]. For the petition I needed to have an estimate of the value of Jim's assets, and note the amounts owing, if any had mortgages or loans;

4.3 *Affidavit of Witness* [exhibit no. 5] **to be sworn and signed by one of the witnesses of Jim's will that Jim had signed the will in the presence of both witnesses.;**

5. **The documents issued by the registrar of probate were:**

5.1 *Certificate of Probate* [exhibit no. 7] **signed by the registrar, stating that probate had been granted to me as executrix;**

5.2 *Certified Certificate of Probate* [exhibit no. 8], **and official copies of the certificate.** I got six copies so I would have extras to give to any institutions requiring proof that I was the executor;

5.3 *Letters Testamentary* [exhibit no. 9] **which also stated that I was the executrix.** It had a copy of the probated will attached, which proved useful. I got a certified copy too in case it was needed;

5.4 *Warrant of Appraisement* [exhibit no. 10A], **appointing the two people I told the registrar would appraise the inventory of Jim's estate.;**

5.5 *Appraisement of Inventory* [exhibit no. 10B] **to be completed with valuations as of the date Jim died, and returned to the registrar within the three months;**

6. **Had *The Royal Gazette* publish an estate notice** [exhibit no. 12] **to inform any of Jim's creditors that his estate had been opened and that I was the executrix;**

7. **Opened chequing account in the estate name. Had bank send monthly statements and keep cancelled cheques.** Service charges for having cheques returned are higher, and photocopies can be obtained if needed to prove a payment;

8. **Set up a filing system for estate documents, tax returns, receipts, etc.;**

9. **Kept a continuing record of all money received and paid out from start to finish.** [exhibits 16A and 16B];

10. **Collected life insurance policies and checked Jim's desk, credit cards, business associations, safety deposit box, and employer for policies;**

11. **Used registered letters to record dates of delivery of documents, payment of legacies, etc.;**

12. **Had lawyer prepare a special agreement to clarify my continued use of the Chester Basin cottage** [exhibit no. 17];

13. **Had the Warrant of Appraisement and Appraisement of Inventory documents completed and returned to registrar. Attached a detailed listing of inventory valuations** [exhibit no.10A with schedule A];

14. **Jim's final tax return** [exhibit no. 20] **for period from January 1 to May 24 was prepared and the tax paid;**

15. **A *Request for Clearance Certificate*** [exhibit no 22] **was filled out after Revenue Canada's notice of assessment for Jim's final income tax return arrived;**

16. **Filed trust income tax and information return** [exhibit no. 24] **for the estate and paid the tax;**

17. **When I received Revenue Canada's clearance certificate** [exhibit no. 25] **which recorded that he did not have any unpaid taxes, I requested an appointment with the registrar to close the estate;**

18. **Had Petition to Close** [exhibit no. 26A], **and Affidavit** [exhibit no. 26B] **provided to registrar to confirm the appointment;**

19. **Had Citation to Close** [exhibit no. 28] **provided to the registrar to be signed by her confirming the date, place, and time of my appearance before the court to close the estate.** After the citation was signed by the registrar I had to send copies to the beneficiaries and any others with an interest in the estate;

20. **Had the Royal Gazette advertise under Citation Notices** [exhibit no. 30] **the estate's closing date, time, and place;**

21. **Had accountant prepare a complete accounting summary of all transactions, starting from the appraisers' inventory valuation, and headed Final Account of Mary Fraser, Executrix** [exhibit no. 31]. I was required to send copies to beneficiaries and anyone else with an interest in the estate;

22. **Signed Executor's Affidavit** [exhibit no. 33] **stating I had made the required notifications to those interested in the estate, telling them the date, time, and place of closing;**

23. **Completed Executor's Final Account** [exhibit no. 34], **to which my accounting report** [exhibit no. 31] **was attached.** I had to swear it was correct at the closing after the registrar had completed her inquiries regarding my administration and was satisfied that it had been done correctly;

24. **The Final Decree** [exhibit no. 36] **was signed and sealed by the registrar, recording that the court was satisfied with my accounting and administration of the estate;**

25. **Paid all donations, gifts, bills, fees, and legacies, and finally paid what was left to the residual heirs and beneficiaries. Then I closed the bank account.** I plan to keep all estate documents in my files for at least seven years.

Mary decided that going over this list with Elizabeth and Chris would provide a good occasion for finding out whether they had made their own wills. Had Elizabeth and her husband appointed someone to be guardian(s) of their children if something should happen to them? Mary thought they should also talk about her giving one or both of them acting together an enduring power of attorney (see glossary) in case she became incapacitated and needed someone to look after her affairs. She had complete confidence in their integrity and knew she would have no cause for concern, by appointing both of them her attorney, to jointly sign her name to papers and documents. Also, she knew they had sufficient business experience and the good common sense to be co-executors of her will. She hoped they will agree to accept the appointment.

T his chapter lists the courts in each province and territory and the principal statutes applicable to probating wills, intestates (those who die without a will), powers of attorney, and mentally incompetent persons, and describes where consolidation copies of these statutes can be obtained. The publications mentioned contain extensive data, from which a few points have been selected to give a brief idea of the contents. In most of the publications, amendments to the acts have been incorporated, but the original statutes and regulations might need to be consulted for complete interpretation and application of the law. Included in many acts are references to other statutes which readers may wish to consult for the province or territory where they live. Note that while the legal system allows individuals to represent themselves in proceedings before the courts, there are circumstances in which it would be advisable or necessary to employ a lawyer or experienced paralegal to accompany or represent an executor in this situation.

ALBERTA
Provincial Courts:
• Court of Queen's Bench of Alberta

• Provincial Court of Alberta
• Surrogate Court of Alberta

Copies of the Surrogate Court rules and consolidations of provincial statutes, published in English, can be obtained from:
The Queen's Printer Bookstore
11510 Kingsway Avenue
Edmonton, AB T5G 2Y5
Telephone: (403) 427-4952
or
The Queen's Printer Bookstore
Main Floor, McDougall Centre
455 Sixth Street SW
Calgary, AB T2P 4E8
Telephone (403) 297-6251

The age of majority is 18.
The Administration of Estates Act, 1997:
The Surrogate Court Act, 1995, and The Dependent Adults Act, 1995, Surrogate Rules Package.
The easy to understand Rules Package has 50 pages of rules for the two acts and 200 pages of the forms to be used. Materials included in this package describe the procedure and forms necessary

to administer a deceased's person's estate and the estates of dependent adults and minors. The package describes the circumstances in which the forms for each step are required, and provides excellent "do-it-yourself" information, including a list of executor and administrator duties. A schedule of court fees is included. Included among the sample forms are:

• an application for grant of probate;
• an application for grant of administration (without will).

The Administration of Estates Act contains 64 sections divided into 3 parts. Note the following points:

• Applications for grants of probate and administration are made in judicial districts to the Surrogate Court of Alberta;
• Gifts made under a will to a witness or the spouse of a witness are void. Gifts made to an executor are valid;
• Holograph wills (wills written in the deceased's own hand, with no witness required) are valid in Alberta;
• The types of will used by marines and persons in the military forces are valid. These wills made by the testator while in military service, or at sea and not in a format otherwise required by the province; the testator can also be underage);
• An executor who is not a resident of Alberta must provide a surety bond to the court. If the will appoints co-executors and one of them is a resident, the bond is not required;
• Notices to claimants of an estate must be advertised in a newspaper published or circulated where the deceased usually lived;
• Compensation paid to a personal representative, unless stated in the will, is fixed by the court, which recognizes the extent of work, the expertise required to complete administrative duties, and any additional work that had to be done.

A "personal representative" is an executor of a will, or an administrator or trustee of an estate;
• Compensation for lawyers is subject to the approval of the court;
• A schedule of court fees is included with the rules;
• Non-resident administrators and executors must provide surety bonds.

The Intestate Succession Act of Alberta specifies to whom the assets of intestates are to be distributed. The Powers of Attorney Act, 1991 contains seventeen sections and a schedule headed, "Notes on the Enduring Power of Attorney."

• "Attorney" means a person who is empowered to act on behalf of the donor under a power of attorney, not necessarily a lawyer. "Donor" means a person who gives a power of attorney;
• The requirements needed for an enduring power of attorney to be valid are contained in the Act. According to the act, it can be made to come into effect at a future time, under definite circumstances specified in the Act,
• The court, on request, can require the attorney to present an account of all transactions made under an enduring power of attorney.

BRITISH COLUMBIA
Provincial Courts:
• Court of Appeal of British Columbia
• Supreme Court of British Columbia
• Provincial Court of British Columbia

Copies of provincial statutes are published in English and can be obtained from:
Crown Publications Inc
521 Fort Street
Victoria, BC V8W 1E7
Telephone (250) 386-4636; Fax (250) 386-0221

The age of majority is 19.

The Estates Administration Act, 1996, is under the jurisdiction of the Supreme Court or a judge of the Supreme Court in communities throughout the province. The Act contains 125 sections and is divided into 13 parts, headed:

Part 1– General

Part 2– Grants of Administration (includes "remuneration to administrators" information).

Part 3– Revocation and Renunciation

Part 4– Discharge of Personal Representatives

Part 5– Official Administrators

Part 6– Proof of Wills in Solemn Form

Part 7– Powers, Duties, and Liabilities of Executors and Administrators

Part 8– Provision for Common-Law Spouses

Part 9– Devolution of Real Estate

Part 10–Distribution of Intestate Estate

Part 11–Insolvent Estates

Part 12–Procedure and Evidence. Includes a requirement that all original wills proved in British Columbia be forwarded by the registrar of the court where they have been proved, to the registrar of the Supreme Court at Victoria and deposited there for safekeeping. This included the particulars of every probate or letters of administration granted or resealed by the court. (Wills and letters of administration granted outside the province can be resealed to make them valid in the province.) There is also a subsection regarding the opening of safety deposit boxes.

Part 13–Deceased Workers' Wages

The Wills Act and The Wills Variations Act, 1996. The Wills Act contains 44 sections and is divided into 4 parts. The Wills Variations Act contains 15 sections.

Note the following points:

• A will is valid when made by "a member of the Canadian Forces while placed on service under the National Defence Act, or a member of the naval, land, or air force of any member of the British Commonwealth of Nations or any ally of Canada while on active service, or a mariner or seaman at sea in the course of a voyage may, regardless of his or her age, dispose of his real or her real and personal estate by will in writing, signed by the testator at its end or by some other person in the presence of and by the direction of the testator." When a will is signed by the testator a witness is not required, but at least one witness is necessary when the will is not signed by the testator;

• Holograph wills made in British Columbia are not valid, except when made as above;

• A will is revoked by the marriage of the testator, unless there is a declaration in the will that it is made in contemplation of the marriage. The Power of Attorney Act, 1996. The act contains 9 sections. Noteworthy points are:

• The authority of an attorney acting under an enduring power of attorney is not terminated in the event of the donor's mental infirmity provided that the witness to the donor's signature is other than the attorney or the spouse of the attorney;

• Included in the publication is a schedule containing two General Power of Attorney forms, one for the appointment of one attorney and the other for appointing more than one attorney. The wording required to declare that the power of attorney may be exercised during any subsequent mental infirmity of the donor is provided.

Adult Guardianship Act, 1993. The act contains 66 sections divided into 4 parts. Among other things it states who may be appointed as an adult's decision maker or guardian, and the documents to be filed, and who is to be served with them.

MANITOBA

Provincial Courts:

• Court of Queen's Bench for Manitoba

• Provincial judicial centres in Brandon, Dawson, Portage la Prairie, La Pas, St. Bonniface, and Winnipeg.

Provincial statutes are published in English and French and can be obtained from:
Province of Manitoba Publications
Lower Level, 200 Vaughan Street
Winnipeg, MB R3C 1T5
Telephone: (204) 945-3101

The age of majority is 18.

The Court of Queen's Bench Surrogate Practice Act, 1987. The act contains 57 sections. Note the following points:

- Deputy registrars for each judicial centre can serve as depositories for the wills of living persons given to them for safekeeping by people who choose to do so;
- The registrar in Winnipeg is provided with lists of the grants of probate and administration, and every revocation of grant of probate, made at judicial centres;
- Grants of probate or administration may be made by the court in any judicial centre;
- The administration of estates is not granted to a person who is not a habitual resident of Manitoba;
- Notarial wills made in the province of Quebec may be admitted to probate without the original will;
- Where grants of probate or letters of administration have been granted by any other province or territory in Canada, most Commonwealth countries, and the United States, they are made effective in Manitoba if the seal of the court is placed on them.

The Wills Act, 1990, contains 61 sections and is divided into 4 parts:

- Holograph wills are valid;
- Military forces and mariner's wills are valid;
- With some exceptions a person's will is revoked by his or her marriage, unless it contains a declaration that it was made in contemplation of marriage;
- The effect of a divorce on a will made before the testator's marriage terminated, unless a contrary intention appears in the will, is that any bequest made to the divorced spouse, or the spouse's appointment as executor or trustee are revoked and the will construed as if the divorced spouse has predeceased the testator.

The Intestate Succession Act, 1990. The Act contains 9 sections regarding the issue of who is entitled to receive the estate, including all real and personal property of an intestate. The status of an adopted child is determined in accordance with the provisions of the Child and Family Services Act.

The Powers of Attorney and Mental Health Amendment Act, 1966. The act contains 29 sections in 4 parts. The parts are:

- Definitions and Application
- Powers of Attorney Generally
- Springing Powers of Attorney
- Enduring Powers of Attorney
- An enduring power of attorney cannot be given by a mentally incompetent, underage, or undischarged bankrupt person;
- A power of attorney can be made to come into force when the mental incompetence of the donor is declared by two medical practitioners, or the occurrence of a specified event.

The Powers of Attorney Act. The act contains 4 sections regarding the powers conveyed by giving someone a power of attorney.

NEW BRUNSWICK
Provincial Courts:

- Court of Appeal of New Brunswick
- Court of Queen's Bench of New Brunswick
- Court of Probate of New Brunswick

Copies of provincial acts published in English and French are listed in a catalogue and can be obtained from:
The Queen's Printer for New Brunswick
Centennial Building Room 115
670 King Street, P.O. Box 6000
Fredericton, NB E3B 5H1
Telephone: (506) 453-2520; Fax: (506) 457-7899

The age of majority is 19.

The Probate Court Act, 1982, amended 1997, and Regulations, 1984/1996. The act contains 80 sections divided into 14 parts. Regulations are divided into 4 parts over 21 pages, followed by 54 pages of blank forms used to probate wills and to apply for administration when there is no will. Two pages specify the applicable amounts of court and solicitor fees. Note the following points:

• The Probate Court of New Brunswick and the judges thereof have jurisdiction over all the estates of deceased persons with property located in the province;

• Sittings of the court take place wherever a probate office is established or where the judge directs;

• An inventory valuation is to be delivered to the clerk of the court within two months after the will is probated or letters of administration granted;

• The family and heirs of a person dying without a valid will have two months to apply for administration of the estate, or the Public Administrator will apply for administration;

• Where the term "personal representative" is used it refers to the person who makes application to the court to be appointed the executor of a will; or the administrator of an estate when there is no will; or the administrator of an estate when there is a will but it did not name an executor, or the executor cannot function in that capacity; or the person to be appointed a guardian for someone;

• When there is no will, the person to whom letters of administration are granted is required to give a bond to the court to ensure proper administration of the estate. The court has the power to dispense with a bond;

• The priority for making payments from the assets of an estate is:

(a) funeral expenses

(b) probate fees

(c) solicitor's costs

(d) wages protected under legislation

(e) liabilities incurred by personal representative for estate administration

(f) commission allowed by Court to personal representative;

• While the Act does not require interested parties to employ a lawyer, first-time executors will likely find it helpful to use legal services for document preparation and procedural guidance;

• There are provisions for sealing letters or other legal documents granted by a court of another jurisdiction to make them legal in New Brunswick;

• Executor fees are set by the court at closing and calculated on the value of the whole estate, including real property (real estate), and are not necessarily limited to 5 per cent. They are set at rates which recognize the work done by the executor, and for a small estate 5 per cent may not be reasonable. In calculating the value of real property the amounts of mortgages or other encumbrances are deducted.

The Wills Act, amended 1997. The Act contains 41 sections divided into 2 parts. Note the following points:

• With some exceptions a person's will is revoked by marriage unless made in contemplation of marriage;

• Holograph wills are valid in New Brunswick;

• Military forces' and mariners' forms of wills are valid;

• Notarial wills made in Quebec can be probated.

The Survivorship Act, 1993 contains 8 sections for establishing presumption of survivorship in cases where people die at the same time. The Act can negate survivorship clauses contained in wills.

The Devolution of Estates Act, 1997 contains 38 sections divided into 2 parts. Part 11, "Intestate Succession," details the persons to whom the estates of intestates are to be distributed.

NEWFOUNDLAND

Provincial Courts:

• Court of Appeal of Newfoundland
• Supreme Court of Newfoundland, Trial Division
  Copies of provincial statutes, published in
English, can be obtained from:
The Office of The Queen's Printer
P.O. Box 8700
Prince Phillip Drive
St. John's, NF A1B 4J6
Telephone: (709) 729-3649; Fax: (709) 729-1930

The age of majority is 19.

The Judicature Act Consolidation, 1993 contains 150 sections divided into 8 parts.

"Judicature" means a body responsible for the administration of justice; in other words, a body of judges. Part VI, "Probate and Administration," contains the portion of the act dealing with estate matters. Note the following points:

• Probate courts are Trial Divisions of the Supreme Court of Newfoundland and can grant letters of probate and administration of estates in cases where there is no will. Judicial centres are in Corner Brook, Gander, Grand Bank, Grand Falls, Happy Valley-Goose Bay, and St. John's;
• A central registry is kept in St. John's of all letters of probate, administrations and guardianships granted in the province;
• An administrator of an estate or a guardian is required to give security for the faithful discharge of his or her duties, unless the court orders otherwise.

Part 11, Probate Rule 56, 1991, "Probate Administration and Guardianship Rules" contains 34 sections numbered 56.01 to 56.34, followed by 36 pages of the forms to be used to make court petitions and presentations. In Newfoundland it is estimated that lawyers handle about 90 per cent of probate applications, but the number is decreasing, as more and more people are doing it themselves. The executor's remuneration is fixed by the judge, taking into consideration the amount of work done and how well the administration of the estate was managed. The Rules do not contain a percentage but in general practice the fee does not exceed 5 per cent of the value of the estate, including both personal and real property. Some highlights:

• Grants of letters of administration of estates are made only to residents of Newfoundland;
• All grants of probate or administration are signed by the registrar.

The Wills Act, amended to 1975-76, contains 43 sections divided into 3 parts, followed by a schedule headed "Convention Providing a Uniform Law on the Form of an International Will." Note the following points:

• Holograph wills are valid in Newfoundland;
• Military forces' and mariners forms of wills are valid regardless of age;
• With some exceptions a person's will is revoked by marriage unless made in contemplation of marriage;
• An unborn child is considered to be living at the time of death of the testator, if the child was conceived before the death and is born alive after the death;
• A will is not invalid just because the testator's residence was not in Newfoundland when the will was made, provided it met the requirements of the jurisdiction where he or she was living at the time.

The Intestate Succession Act, 1970, contains 16 sections which state to whom the assets of an intestate are to be distributed. This includes the residue of an estate which is not disposed of by will.

The Enduring Power of Attorney Act, 1990 contains 14 sections concerning the authority given under an enduring power of attorney.

NORTHWEST TERRITORIES

- Courts Court of Appeal of Northwest Territories
- Supreme Court of Northwest Territories

Copies of territory statutes, published in English and French, can be obtained from:

Canartic Graphics Ltd.
P.O. Box 2758, 5102-50th Street
Yellowknife, NWT X1A 2R1
Telephone: (867) 873-5924; Fax: (867) 920-4371

The age of majority is 19.

Probate and intestate rules are included in the Supreme Court Act.

The Intestate Succession Act, 1988 details the persons to whom both the real and personal property of an intestate is to be distributed, and contains 14 sections.

The Wills Act, 1988 contains 27 sections divided into 9 parts. Note the following points:

- Military forces', mariners', and RCMP members' wills are valid regardless of the testator's age;
- Holograph wills are valid;
- The executor named in a will can also be one of the witnesses;
- With some exceptions, a person's will is revoked by marriage unless it was made in contemplation of marriage.
- Power of Attorney. No plans are in place to enact a Power of Attorney Act until after the territory is divided on April 1, 1999.

NOVA SCOTIA

Provincial Courts:

- Court of Appeal of Nova Scotia, Halifax
- Supreme Court of Nova Scotia
  (Provincial Courts include Court of Probate)

Consolidated copies of provincial statutes, published in English, can be obtained from:
Nova Scotia Government Book Store
1700 Granville Street, Halifax, NS B3J 2T3
Telephone (902) 424-7580; Fax (902) 424-5599

The age of majority is 18.

The Probate Act, revised 1989 and amended to 1994-5 contains 165 sections divided into 28 parts, followed by 28 pages of the forms required by the Court of Probate. Probate court services are provided in the following communities: Amherst, Annapolis Royal, Guysborough, Halifax, Kentville, Lunenburg, Pictou, Port Hawkesbury, Sydney, Truro, and Yarmouth. Some highlights of the Act:

- It is not necessary for a person to employ a lawyer to act for him or her in a Court of Probate. Those who so desire may prepare and file any papers themselves, and appear in person and conduct their own cause in court;
- The executor's maximum commission is limited to 5 per cent of the amount of money administered;
- Commission is not paid on real estate unless it has been sold and the money received placed in the estate's bank account;
- A person granted administration of an estate is required to give a bond to the court as security for faithful administration of the estate. Executors receiving grant of probate are not required to provide performance bonds, because their appointments were made by deceased testators. The courts require surety bonds because anyone applying to the court to be appointed to administer an estate does so without having been named by the deceased to perform the duties of his executor;
- Section 41, regarding articles that shall be omitted from the inventory and not considered as assets, is obviously out of date. For example "the wearing apparel of the deceased, not exceeding forty dollars in value, shall be distributed at the discretion of the executor or administrator." A century ago this might have been more meaningful, but today the clothes people are buried in have more value. I have never seen this item listed in an inventory, and court registrars do not even ask about objects of such trivial value;

- The cost of a gravestone or monument, with some qualifications, may be paid by the estate. The Wills Act, revised 1989, contains 34 sections divided into 5 parts. Note the following points:
- With some exceptions a person's will is revoked by marriage unless it was made in contemplation of marriage;
- A will does not become invalid in the event the witness becomes incompetent or deceased and unable to prove execution of the will;
- Holograph wills are not valid in Nova Scotia;
- A will may be invalid if the person appointed executor has signed it as a witness;
- Wills made outside the province, wherever the domicile of the testator at the time of making the will, or at the time of death, as regards personal property (not including real estate), can be admitted to probate in the province if made in accordance with the form required by: (a) the law of Nova Scotia; (b) the law of the place where they were made; (c) the law of the place where the testator was resident when made; (d) the law then in force in the place where the testator had domicile of origin. This does not mean that a holograph will made while the testator lived outside the province can be probated in Nova Scotia;
- Military forces' and mariners' forms of wills are valid;
- Anyone who suppresses a will may incur a fine for each month it is suppressed.

The Intestate Succession Act, revised 1989, states the persons to whom all the assets of an intestate, within the province and outside it, are to be distributed, after the payment of debts, funeral expenses, charges, and administration expenses. Courts of Probate have jurisdiction. Appeals and contentious matters are settled by the Supreme Court of Nova Scotia.

The Incompetent Persons Act, 1972, has not been revised as of the time of the writing. The Trial Division of the Supreme Court, or a judge thereof, has jurisdiction. The Act contains 21 sections divided into 2 parts, headed "Appointment of Guardian" and "Powers and Duties of Guardian." It is necessary to resort to the Act when a person becomes mentally incompetent to manage his own affairs, and has not given someone authorization under an enduring power of attorney to manage them for him or her. Note that it can be expensive to obtain a guardianship appointment from the court.

The Powers of Attorney Act, 1988, contains just 6 sections, mainly dealing with enduring powers of attorney. Note the following points:

- The attorney appointed by the donor can apply to a judge of the Trial Division of the Supreme Court for another person to be the attorney in his place;
- A judge of the Trial Division of the Supreme Court can require the appointed attorney of a legally incapacitated donor to present an accounting of the donor's affairs, and other matters.

NUNAVUT TERRITORY

Nunavut is a newly established territory, which was formerly part of the Northwest Territories. Nunavut will initially have the same judicial system as the Northwest Territories, with Iqaluit the capital and seat of government.

ONTARIO

Provincial Courts:

- Court of Appeal for Ontario
- Ontario Court of Justice (General Division)
- Ontario Court of Justice (Provincial Division)
- Ontario Court (General Division)

Copies of provincial statutes, published in English and French can be obtained from:
Publications Ontario Bookstore
1st Floor, 880 Bay Street
Toronto, ON M7A 1N8

Telephone: (416) 326-5300
Toll free: 1-800-668-9938

Ottawa Bookstore
Level 2, 161 Egin St.
Ottawa, ON K2P 2K1
Telephone: (613) 238-3630
Toll free: 1-800-268-8758; Fax: (613) 566-2234

The age of majority is 18.

The Estates Administration Act, 1994, The Succession Law Reform Act, 1994, and The Estates Act, 1993 contain what in some provinces are probate, wills and intestate acts.

The Ontario Court (General Division), with Estates offices in larger communities throughout the province, has jurisdiction. It issues letters of probate with copies of the will attached and letters of administration where there is no will. When the executor appointed by the testator cannot act, the court will issue letters of administration with will attached. The Ontario Court can also appoint guardians of both persons and property.

The Estates Administration Act contains 28 sections followed by 3 forms of affidavit. Note the following points:

- "Personal representative" means an executor, an administrator, or an administrator with the will attached to the appointment document;
- A personal representative is required to search for children born outside marriage;
- Distribution of the estate of an intestate is not to be made until one year after the administrator has been appointed;
- Many sections deal with real estate transactions.

The Estates Act contains 53 sections. Note the following points:

- The registrar at local offices of the Ontario Court (General Division) serves as a depository of the wills of living people, kept there for safekeeping;
- All registrars provide details of all grants of probate, administration, and related matters to the office of the estate registrar of Ontario, where a central registry is maintained;
- Letters of administration are not granted to persons not residing in Ontario;
- Letters of probate are not granted to persons not resident in Ontario, or elsewhere in the Commonwealth, unless the person has given a security bond. The judge can dispense with the bond or reduce the amount;
- The persons to whom administration of an intestacy may be granted are listed;
- The types of wills made by members of Canada's military forces and sailors are valid, regardless of the testator's age;
- Holograph wills are valid;
- A notarial will made in Quebec can be probated without presentation of the original will.

The Succession Law Reform Act contains 79 sections. Three of note are:

- Testate Succession Intestate Succession
- Designation of Beneficiaries of Interest in Funds or Plans
- Survivorship Support of Dependents

Note the following points:

- With some exceptions a will made by a person under 18 years of age is not valid;
- With some exceptions a person's will is revoked by marriage unless it was made in contemplation of marriage. Bequests made to divorced or separated spouses may be presumed to be invalid unless the will states otherwise.

A powers of attorney booklet is available from The Public Guardian and Trustee, 595 Bay Street, Toronto, Ontario, M5G 2M6 and contains instructions and forms for a continuing power of attorney for property and a power of attorney for personal care. It reflects amendments to the Substitute Decisions Act, 1992. Giving someone authority to your personal care deserves serious consideration. The booklet provides very helpful information on the subject.

PRINCE EDWARD ISLAND
Provincial Courts:
- Supreme Court of Prince Edward Island
- Appeal Division of the Supreme Court of Prince Edward Island
- Estates Section of the Trial Division of the Supreme Court of PEI

Copies of provincial statutes, published in English, can be obtained from:
Prince Edward Island Information Service
PO Box 2000
Charlottetown, PEI C1A 7N8
Telephone: (902) 368-4000; Fax: (902) 368-5544

The age of majority is 18.

The Probate Act and May 1994 amendment to the Probate Act contain 129 sections divided into 6 parts: general provisions, procedure, distribution of estates of intestates, wills, devolution of real property, international wills. Note the following points:

- Probate court is the Supreme Court of Prince Edward Island—Estates Section;
- If the assets of an estate are insufficient to pay all the debts of the deceased, the priority of payments is listed and funeral expenses are not to exceed $1,500;
- When an executor dies before the estate is settled, the executor of his or her will does not automatically become the executor of the first testator's will, but he or she may apply for administration;
- The cost of a gravestone and payment needs the judge's written consent to be charged to the estate. An amount can be set aside for care of the grave in perpetuity at the discretion of the court;
- A resident named in a will as executor has thirty days from the time of being informed he or she was so named to cause the will to be proved, apply for probate, or refuse executorship;
- A non-resident has three months to do likewise.

There are penalties if the appointees do not comply;
- Letters of probate or administration granted in other provinces, or in any part of the Commonwealth, can be sealed by the court and thereby made to have the full force and effect as if they had originally been granted in Prince Edward Island;
- No will made by an unmarried person under the age of eighteen is valid;
- In the case of a person who witnessed the signing of a will and who is also a beneficiary, or whose wife or husband is a beneficiary, the legacy is void;
- An "Executor" may be a witness to the execution (i.e. the signing or testation) of the will;
- A person's will is revoked by marriage unless it is made in contemplation of marriage;
- Holograph wills are not valid;
- A wife or husband living in adultery does not receive any share of his or her spouse's estate in an intestacy;
- Military forces' and mariners' wills are valid regardless of the testator's age;
- The Act states to whom the net value of the estate of an intestate is to be distributed;
- The Act does not require interested parties to employ lawyers;
- There are provisions for proving and granting probate for a will which was executed outside the province. This gives an executor the authority to administer the deceased's assets located within the province;
- A personal representative is not permitted to profit from the estate, but the court may allow a commission on the gross amount received in the estate of up to 5 per cent, over and above his necessary expenses.

The Powers of Attorney Act, 1988, contains ten sections in two parts and a schedule containing an acceptable power of attorney form. The schedule contains a paragraph which can be added to the form to make it an enduring power of attorney. The donee of a power of attorney acting for the donor during the donor's legal incapacity can be required to file his accounts for approval of transactions done in the donor's name. This must be done with the prothontary of the Supreme Court.

QUEBEC

Provincial Courts:

• Court of Appeal of Quebec
• Superior Court of Quebec
• Court of Quebec and its judicial districts

The provincial offices where information, published in English and French, and copies of the Civil Code can be obtained are listed in telephone books. For English publications contact:
le Ministère de la Justice
Direction des Communications
1200 route de L'Eglise
Sainte-Foy, QC G1V 4M1
Telephone: (418) 643-5140; Fax: (418) 646-4449
E-mail: justice.gouv.qc.ca
Web site: http://www.justice.gouv.qc.ca

The age of majority is 19.

The Civil Code of Quebec, 1997-1998. The Province of Quebec in 1992 legislated an act respecting the implementation of the Civil Code. The 1997-1998 edition is written in French with English translation appearing beside the French for most of the text. The Civil Code is the backbone of the law in Quebec.

Civil status of death: When anyone dies the "act of death" must be reported in a declaration of death completed by either the deceased's spouse, a close relative, or, failing them, any other person who is able to identify the deceased. The declaration is sent to the Registrar of Civil Status, with a copy of the attestation of death, completed by a physician or two peace officers. It is then possible to obtain copies of the "act of death" document from the registrar for proof of death which is needed to open the estate and determine the day on which various benefit plans begin or cease.

Pamphlets and other sources of information about the declaration of death can be obtained from:
la Direction de l'Etat Civil
Ministère de la Justice
205 rue Montmagy
Quebec, PQ G1N 2Z9
Telephone (418): 643-3900, fax (418) 644-0476.

Wills: A pamphlet issued by the Ministry of Justice concerns exercising your rights regarding the disposal of your body; whether, for example, you want to donate organs. The leaflet suggests that wishes be recorded in a separate document left where it can be read immediately after your death, rather than in a will. (Usually the contents of a will are not disclosed until a few days after death, by which time the body may already have been cremated or buried.) Note the following points:

• Rights of the surviving spouse cannot be limited if he or she remarries;
• Holograph wills are valid and must be written entirely in the testator's hand, or toes or mouth if he is handicapped. Witnesses are not required, and the will is valid even if it is undated;
• A will made in the presence of two witnesses may be drawn up by the testator or someone else. If you sign the will yourself, the suggested testimoum clause is, "Signed by [name of testator] and recognized by him as being his own signature affixed to his will in the presence together of the testator and at his request." If you have someone else sign for you the suggested clause is, "Signed by [name of the person who signed for you], at the request and in the presence of [name of testator], and recognized by the latter as being his signature affixed to his will in the presence together of the undersigned

witnesses, which witnesses have signed in the presence of the testator." In both examples the witnesses sign below the testator's signature. Witnesses must be of full age and if they are named as legatees, their bequest is null and void;

- A notarial will is one drawn up by a notary and requires two witnesses. These wills, while more expensive, have many advantages. The notary keeps the original will and the testator is given a copy. Unlike the other two forms of will, a notarial will does not need to be probated;
- Wills of living persons, when left with lawyers, are entered in a register of wills maintained by the Bar of Quebec. Notarial wills are entered in the register maintained by the Chambre des Notaries du Québec;
- Holographs wills and wills not made by notaries are probated in Superior Courts, which appoint liquidators to administer and liquidate estates;
- "Liquidator" is the position previously referred to as "testamentary executor";
- Wills in languages other than French or English require translations to accompany them when presented for probate.

Successions: The Civil Code of Quebec determines the persons who are entitled to share in the distribution of the estate of an intestate, and the portion for each person. Liquidation and distribution of estate assets in cases where the deceased did not appoint a liquidator in a will can be done in several ways. The heirs can act together or designate a person who is not an heir to perform the duties of liquidator. They may choose a liquidator, without any formalities, by making a simple declaration in writing and signing it; or they may ask the Supreme Court to appoint an acting liquidator. To obtain a copy of a brochure dealing with such matters, contact the Ministere of Justice in Sainte-Foy (see above).

- Quebec income tax returns are required to be prepared for deceased persons and filed with the Ministere du Revenue du Québec.
- Tutorship (Guardianship), personal care, and related topics are covered in the Civil code.

SASKATCHEWAN
Provincial Courts:
- Court of Appeal of Saskatchewan
- Her Majesty's Court of Queen's Bench for Saskatchewan
- Provincial Court of Saskatchewan
  Copies of provincial statutes published in English, and some in French, can be obtained from:
Saskatchewan Justice, Office of The Queen's Printer
1871 Smith Street
Regina, SK S4P 3V7
Telephone: (306) 787-6894; Fax: (306) 787-9779

The age of majority is 18.

The Trustee Act, 1997, Chapter T23, is an act respecting trustees, executors, and the administration of estates. The act contains 87 sections divided into 21 parts. Note the following points:

- "Trustee" includes an executor or administrator of an estate;
- Several sections deal with taking money from an infant's fund for his support where it is held by an executor or administrator under various circumstances, commencing with Section 52;
- An executor, administrator, or guardian appointed by the court is entitled to such fair and reasonable allowance for his work as allowed by the court or a judge.

The Queen's Bench Act, revised to 1996, has 142 sections divided into 36 parts. Sections 100 to 142 deal with matters related to probate and the administration of estate. Note the following points:

- The Court of Queen's Bench has jurisdiction and the province constitutes one judicial district.

Judicial centres are established by regulations in places where, at least one judge resides. In 1996 there were 13 judicial centres, listed in the publication The Queen's Bench Judges Residence Regulations;

- When someone dies without having made a will, or if there is a will but the executor named in the will is unable or unwilling to act, some person interested in the estate can make application to the court to be appointed administrator. The court may grant the applicant letters of administration if there is no will; or letters of administration with will annexed if there is one; and may state whether the grant is for general, special, or limited purposes;
- "Trustee" includes an executor or administrator;
- Classes of securities in which trustees may invest are listed;
- An executor's or administrator's fee may be set by the court or a judge unless it is fixed in the will. An estate is a trust and the executor or administrator the trustee of it;
- Bequests made to divorced or separated spouses are presumed invalid unless the will states otherwise;
- With few exceptions, every person to whom letters of administration are granted is required to give surety bonds to the court. Persons who are executors of probated wills are not required to give surety bonds;
- Local registrars' offices serve as depositories for wills of living persons.

The Wills Act, 1992, contains 42 sections divided into 3 parts, plus a schedule regarding international wills. Some points deserving special mention:

- Holograph wills are valid, and "handwriting" includes mouthwriting;
- A married person under eighteen years of age can make a valid will. Also, a person in the armed forces or a mariner or seaman can make a valid will while under eighteen;
- With some exceptions a person's will is revoked by marriage unless it was made in contemplation of marriage;
- A change of domicile of a person does not invalidate a will made before the change.

The Intestate Succession Act details to whom the real and personal property of an intestate is to be distributed.

The Powers of Attorney Act, 1996, contains 5 sections, printed on one page. Section 3 states that the authority given by a written power of attorney does not terminate when the donor becomes mentally infirm, provided the document states the authority is to continue notwithstanding any mental infirmity. If the document does not contain such a clause, the attorney's authority ceases in the event the donor becomes mentally infirm.

YUKON TERRITORY
Territory Courts:
- Court of Appeal of Yukon Territory
- Supreme Court of Yukon Territory

Copies of territory statutes, published in English and French, can be obtained from:
Yukon Government Services,
Queen's Printer Section
P.O. Box 2703
Whitehorse, YK Y1A 2C6
Telephone: (867) 667-5783; Fax: (867) 393-6210.

The age of majority is 19.

Probate of Wills: the Yukon has adopted British Columbia's probate laws, which the Supreme Court of Yukon Territory interprets and applies to grant probate of wills and letters of administration. Some Yukon statutes dealing with wills and estate matters are: The Wills Act, 1986, contains 29 sections divided into 6 parts. Note the following points:

- Holograph wills are valid;
- The executor named in a will can be one of its witnesses;

- With some exceptions a person's will is revoked by marriage unless it was made in contemplation of marriage;
- Wills made outside the Yukon can be valid for probate in the Yukon.

The Intestate Succession Act, 1986, contains 20 sections, stating to whom both the real and personal property of an intestate is to be distributed. Note the following points:

- A spouse living in adultery at the time of an intestate's death receives nothing from the deceased's estate;
- Descendants and relatives, begotten before an intestate's death but born thereafter, inherit as if they were born before his death and survived him.

The Dependants Relief Act, 1986, contains 22 sections. Note the following points:

- "Deceased" means a testator who has made a will or a person dying intestate;
- Dependants of a deceased include a person divorced from the deceased for up to three years prior to his death; and a person of the opposite sex living with but not legally married to the deceased for at least the previous three years as his or her spouse, if, in both cases, they were dependent on the deceased for maintenance and support;
- Where a deceased has not made adequate provision for the proper maintenance and support of his or her dependants, the Supreme Court has the power to order that adequate provision be made by his estate;
- Bank deposits in the deceased's name in trust, deposits in joint accounts, and real estate registered with another person as tenants in common can be added into the capital value of the estate and included as testamentary disposals, for the purpose of the Act.

The Enduring Power of Attorney Act, 1995, contains 22 sections followed by a schedule headed, "Notes on the Enduring Power of Attorney," and an admonition to donors to "read these notes before signing this document." Included in the requirements to be satisfied for the document to make it an enduring power of attorney is a lawyer's certificate stating the donor received independent legal advice.

DEPARTMENT OF INDIAN AFFAIRS AND NORTHERN DEVELOPMENT

Jurisdiction and authority for a deceased Registered (Status) Indian's estate is vested exclusively in the Department of Indian Affairs and Northern Development. Correspondence should be sent to:
The Minister, Indian Affairs and
Northern Development
Ottawa, ON K1A 0H4

Government of Canada forms are issued on behalf of the minister by the regional director general. The documents are: appointment of administrator, approval of will, and approval of will and appointment of administrator with will annexed, for use when the executor appointed by the testator cannot apply or fails to apply to probate the will.

XII

TYPES OF WILLS AND HOW TO MAKE ONE

No one argues against the idea that everyone, except perhaps unmarried minors, should have a will and keep it updated. The trick is to do it. For some people the problem of deciding who gets what and who is to be the executor is difficult, so they do nothing until getting close to their last days. Estates generally are not tangled or difficult to administer except when the deceased has not made a valid last will. When that happens, an application has to be made to a court asking it to appoint someone to fulfil the role of executor or liquidator to take charge of all assets and distribute them according to provincial or territorial laws.

It would be much easier if every adult made a will. For most of us it is a simple process and easily done. Exceptions are those with extensive assets located in various provinces and countries, who therefore require expert legal, accounting, and taxation advice. Planning and drafting wills in such situations is very important. Undoubtedly the late K. C. Irving spent a lot of time and money designing ways to have his last will and testament keep his very substantial oil and industrial empire together after he died.

In Canada a legally valid form of will is generally called a formal will. It can be typed or handwritten but must be signed at the bottom by the testator and two witnesses, all of whom must be present and sign at the same time. Estate-related statutes in all provinces and territories accept executor (or liquidator) appointments made by wills which have been granted probate in other provinces and territories. For example, the executor of a holographic will probated in Saskatchewan can have the probate court in Nova Scotia place its seal on the probated documents, thereby giving the executor authority to act for the estate in Nova Scotia. This process is called "resealing." Provinces and territories also can reseal wills which have been granted probate in the United Kingdom and other Commonwealth countries; and some accept the probate of other countries as well, including the United States.

Wills prepared in Quebec by notaries are an anomaly in cases where the will is to be probated in another province or territory because the notary retains the original will that does not have to be probated in Quebec. The notaries provide copies of wills to other jurisdictions when they need to be probated. Letters of verification are issued in Quebec for other forms of will for which probate has been granted and liquidators appointed.

Courts grant probate of wills regardless of who has prepared them, as long as they meet the province's or territory's legal requirements. After all, a will is simply a statement made in writing by someone who intends it to be acted upon after his or her death. Probate courts endeavour to accommodate the process as much as legally possible. However, wills should be prepared in a format acceptable in the province where the maker lives; otherwise, there may be difficulties having it successfully probated. To be confident that the courts will accept and grant probate of a formal will, it must meet a number of basic requirements. The following is an explanation of some key terms:

Formal Will: Document signed by the testator or testatrix containing instructions which become effective when the person dies. The will made by James Fraser (Exhibit no. 2) is an example of a formal will. The testator's full name and place of residence must be stated.

Declaration: Statement that this is the testator's last will and testament and that it revokes all former wills.

Gender Clause: Used when people of both genders are named in the will. For instance, if alternate executors of both genders were appointed, the gender clause might read: "The term 'executor' refers to my executor or executors as the case may be and any reference to my executor in the singular form shall be deemed to include the plural form and where importing any gender shall be deemed to include the other gender."

Executor or Executrix: The person, persons, institution, or any combination thereof who are to follow the instructions in the will. Provision should be made for alternate executors to administer an estate in the event that the original executor is unable or unwilling to act when the testator dies. In most jurisdictions, if an executor dies while administering an estate, the executor of his will becomes responsible for administering both estates, unless he declines to do so. Executors named in wills who are not residents of the same province or territory as the testator may encounter probate difficulties and may have to post a security bond; therefore, it is recommended that a testator choose an executor who lives in the same province or territory.

Co-executors: It is not uncommon for a person to appoint two or more people to be co-executors of his will. In some instances this is done for business reasons, to ensure that the terms of the will are followed closely and the estate assets efficiently taken care of. In other instances co-executors are chosen to provide an executor spouse the support of someone who may be more experienced in such matters. Also, having two executors reduces the chance of one of them being dead or unwilling to serve as executor when the testator dies. Probate courts prefer that at least one of the executors is a resident of the testator's province or territory.

Directions to executor: Instructions to the executor on how to pay debts, taxes, funeral, and testamentary expenses for administering the estate. "Taxes" include income tax, estate taxes, property taxes, and provincial taxes. There are no succession taxes in Canada at the time of writing.

Bequests, legacies, donations, gifts, devises: Words used in stating the amounts of money and real and personal property is to be distributed from the estate. The words all mean the same thing except "devise," which denotes a transfer of ownership of real estate. Consideration should be given in some instances to the disposition of gifts meant for specific beneficiaries in the event one or more of them dies before the testator.

Common disaster and survival clause: The use of these clauses should be considered, because accidents and other misfortunes occasionally result in the simultaneous death of both spouses. While it is considered in some jurisdictions that the younger spouse is assumed to have been the second to die, applicable statutes are at variances in this regard. Clause 5 of James Fraser's will had a common disaster provision that if his wife did not survive him by fifteen days or more, she would receive nothing from his estate.

Residue: Whatever is left in an estate after all expenses and specific gifts and legacies have been paid, and all money collected. The residue consists of all undistributed assets of every kind. The testator must supply directions to the executor regarding what is to be done with the residue. If the will does not state to whom the residue of an estate is to go, the province's or territory's intestate act will take over and choose the persons to whom it is to be given.

Trusts: An estate is a testamentary trust, and the executor is the trustee for it. Most estates are settled and closed in the usual fashion in less than two years. However, there are situations where the testator has his estate hold back some of its assets for distribution for a specific purpose. For instance, the fund could be used over time to provide personal care for an alcoholic, incompetent, or underage relative. It is important to obtain expert legal and income tax advice when setting up a trust. Guidance is needed in such matters as deciding who should be the trustee, what assets should be placed in the trust, how and when will the beneficiary receive trust payments and for how long, and so on.

Registered Retirement Savings Plans: A will should state the person who is the beneficiary of any RRSP and RRIF pension plans owned by the testator. Ideally, the beneficiary designation is made at institutions holding the accounts when the plans are opened; however, it is a good idea to name the beneficiary again in a will. While the owner of RRSP or RRIF plans can name anyone beneficiary, it is only when the beneficiary is the spouse that the plan's assets can pass to him or her

free of income tax. The purpose of RRSP and RRIF plans is to become retirement income funds, providing support to the contributor and/or his spouse in their retirement years. The fact that monies withdrawn from RRSP and RRIF plans are considered taxable income is understandable in view of the fact that no tax is paid on money when it was placed in them, or on the interest, dividends, and capital gains earned by the money.

There are serious income tax consequences to be considered if one appoints a party other than a spouse as the beneficiary of an RRSP or RRIF. For example, if the deceased had $200,000 in his RRSP or RRIF, and the beneficiary was his or her daughter, the tax bite could be nearly half, i.e. $100,000. The question then is, "Who pays the income tax? Is it deducted from the money paid to the beneficiary, or does the estate pay it?" If the owner's will names the beneficiary of his or her retirement plans and states that the payment is to be less the portion of income taxes applicable thereon, then the beneficiary receives tax-paid dollars without personal tax implications, and the estate is not stuck without the money to pay the tax.

Executor investment and other powers: These enable the executor to invest estate money as he or she thinks best without restrictions from provincial trustee laws. Also, they enable the executor to use his or her valuation of assets when dealing with anyone interested in the estate. This could be important, for example, in selling items such as coin and stamp collections, or delivering to heirs items such as antiques and paintings. In James Fraser's will, clause 10 authorized his executor to value any estate assets in her uncontrolled discretion, and made her valuations binding upon anyone interested in the estate. Revenue Canada and probate courts are not bound by the clauses.

Guardian appointment: If the testator has minor-age children, he or she should appoint a person or persons to care for them as their guardian until they reach the age of majority. Potential guardians should be consulted before they are appointed. Sometimes two guardians are appointed, one for property and the other for the children. If a guardian is appointed for the children and not for their property, the executor will normally serve as trustee for their property. In that case the estate's testamentary trust would not be closed until all children had reached maturity.

Mortgaged real estate: If the testator plans to devise (give) real property, it should be clearly stated whether or not any mortgage remains on it, and if so, whether it is to be paid, in part or in full, by the estate.

Testimoum clause: The final clause in a will, where the testator states that it is his or her last will and signs in the presence of two witnesses. (See exhibit no. 2 for an example of an acceptable clause.) The two witnesses must be adults, neither of them should be beneficiaries under the will, and above their signatures there should be a dated statement that all three of them were in the presence of each other when they signed. The witnesses' names and addresses should be placed below their signatures. When it comes time to prove the will for probate, at least one of the witnesses will have to complete an affidavit stating that all three of them signed the will at the same time. There can be exceptions to this process when both witnesses are deceased or cannot be located when the time comes to prove the will. Legislation and the courts have procedures to deal with these and other unusual situations. It does not matter how much time has passed since a will was made; if it is the last one the testator made, it can be probated.

Codicil: (See exhibit no. 37 for an example of a codicil.) The testator can make amendments or additions to his or her will such as changing executors, adding or deleting a beneficiary, increasing bequests, and so on, by the use of a codicil. A codicil must state that it is a codicil to the testator's last will and testament, identify it by date, and be executed with the same formalities as a formal will, however it is not necessary to have the same two witnesses who signed the formal will. When the time comes for the will and codicil to be presented for probate, the witnesses to the codicil can be the only ones required to prove both it and the will. Both are read together and the courts, when granting probate, refer to both in their documents appointing executors, liquidators, estate representatives, and estate trustees.

Wills by minors: People under eighteen or nineteen years of age, depending on where they reside, cannot make valid wills unless they are or have been married, or are planning to marry. An exception is made for minors in the military or navy. From the caselaw it appears that a single underage parent cannot make a valid will.

Unofficial memorandum clause: We all have some personal possessions we would like to give to specific friends and family members when we die. Without imposing any legal obligations on our executor, we can ask him or her to dispose of such items for us by writing an informal memorandum. Such a memorandum ideally should be placed with the will or other important papers and, though not legally binding, it can help avoid disputes about who gets certain items. For instance, an aunt might want a niece to have certain articles of clothing, another niece to have a favourite chair, and someone else to have her china. When such items have little monetary value, her executors would give the articles as requested and not include them in the estate's inventory. However, if the items had more than nominal cash values, the executors would have to consider the rights of residual heirs.

Living wills: These are something quite different from the normal sort of will treated in this book. Living wills record people's wishes regarding the kind and extent of medical treatment they wish or do not wish to receive in the event they are no longer able to communicate. Living wills may not be legally recognized in all provinces and territories. Individuals should discuss the subject with their family, doctor, and lawyer.

Exhibit no. 38 is a copy of a living will published a few years ago by an organization called Concern For Dying (250 West 57th Street, New York, N.Y. 10019). While it may not have legal standing in the health care system, it covers the basic issues that many of us would be concerned about if we became incapacitated with no reasonable expectation of recovery.

The most important things to keep in mind when making a will are to make sure that it contains all the requirements to make it legally valid in the province or territory where you reside, and that it is easily understood and written in plain language. Read it over several times to make sure anyone reading it will clearly understand what you want done with all your assets. Make sure the wording does not have more than one interpretation. For instance, do not make bequests to "my children"—name them. Otherwise, the executor cannot be sure that the only children you parented are the ones in your present family. Also, a provision should be made for the possibility that you may outlive some or all of the beneficiaries named in your will; always state to whom the executor is to distribute the residue of your estate. Probate and intestate acts require executors and administrators to place notices in the *Royal Gazette* or other publications for the purpose of publicly advertising that an estate has been opened. Once executors and administrators of estates have followed the required court processes, fully completed their administrative duties, had their accounts accepted and received court consent to close the estates, anyone subsequently filing a claim against the estate is simply too late and will not make a successful claim. It should further be noted that parents do not have a responsibility to make bequests to children who have reached majority, but do have a responsibility to provide for infant children in their wills. This sometimes includes underage children who were born unbeknownst to their father.

Unless you reside in a province or territory where court registrars provide a safekeeping depository service for the wills of living persons, the best place to keep your will is in a safety deposit box. Keep a copy at home and periodically review it to consider whether any changes should be made. You may wish to make additions or deletions, change your executor, or have your will rewitnessed if the original witnesses have died, become mentally incompetent or have become unreachable. In such circumstances it is quite easy to simply prepare an update of the old will and get two competent witnesses who are not beneficiaries to meet with you and sign it. There is no requirement for an executor or witness to read or be informed of the contents of the will, but the executor should have an understanding of what the estate is like, where the banking is done, and what is expected of him or her. A mentally handicapped person is not necessarily prohibited from being a witness to a will. Some jurisdictions allow an executor to also be a witness, but witnesses are very unlikely to be permitted to receive any legacies from the estate.

A will is automatically revoked when the testator marries, unless there is a declaration in the will stating it was made in contemplation of the marriage. Otherwise, a new will made after the marriage is required. If no new will is made the estate will be distributed in accordance with intestate succession laws and not as planned in the voided will.

In some provinces it is required by law that witnesses and the testator initial each page of the will. This reduces the risk of pages of the will being removed and replaced. This is a recommended precaution even in provinces where it is not legally required.

Funeral planning: An increasing number of people make plans for their own funerals by making their wishes known in a written record. Testators may state the kind of church service they want, including the hymns to be sung, and so on. The funeral home might even be chosen by the testator. When definite plans are made in this manner, family members and executors are relieved from the stress of having to make the numerous decisions involved under already stressful conditions. Exhibit no. 1 is an example of a funeral director's working file, which gives an idea of the amount of information funeral homes need for burials and cremations. It is not necessary to wait until death is imminent to plan your own funeral.

Funeral homes often offer prepaid funeral packages making it possible to settle all arrangements, including limousine services, chapel services, and casket purchase. It is possible to fully prepay funeral contracts so there will be no additional charges no matter how long the "client" lives. Prepaid funeral plans are governed by provincial statutes which require that the money used to pay for them be placed in trust accounts until the death of the client.

XIII

INTESTATE SUCCESSIONS

A person's estate is an intestacy when a will does not exist or cannot be found or when a will is found but has not been properly made and cannot be probated.

When no papers resembling a will can be located, or those found are not acceptable for probate, the only way to deal with the deceased's assets is to have someone apply to the court to be appointed administrator of the estate. When this happens, the opportunity for the deceased to have the assets distributed as he or she would have liked is lost. Succession laws take over and completely direct how distribution is to be made.

Anyone dying without a valid will may cause serious and legal and financial problems for family members and heirs. Estate distribution rules are inflexible and assets can easily be tied up for months until legal formalities (and possibly challenges) have been satisfied.

"Letters of Administration" is the name commonly given to the documents in which courts appoint administrators, trustees, or personal representatives to take charge of the properties of an intestate with a view to settling the estate. Will-related terminology varies from province to province. In Quebec the person appointed is called the liquidator. In Ontario the document is called the "Certificate of Appointment of Estate Trustee Without a Will." The duties and responsibilities of court-appointed trustees, personal representatives, liquidators, and administrators are the same as those of executors, except that the courts are much more involved. Wills appoint executors and courts give legal confirmation to their appointments by granting probate which documents their approval. In an intestacy, except in Quebec, someone has to make application to the court for a grant of administration. The laws in each province and territory dictate who can be appointed to administer an intestate person's properties. The first person entitled to the appointment in all provinces is a spouse, followed by next of kin. Needless to say the person who becomes administrator or liquidator may not be the one best suited for the job, or the person that the deceased would have chosen.

Anyone entitled to apply to be an administrator does not have to do so. Should it happen that the spouse and all kin are found unqualified, the appointment can go to a public trustee. Public trustees are appointed by the government of the province. Public trustees carry out the same duties as estate executors or intestacy administrators and can also be designated as the guardians (tutors in Quebec) of infants and the custodians of the estates of minors.

As mentioned before, administrators of intestate estates have the same duties and responsibilities as executors. They are required to follow the same procedure for filing inventories, income tax returns, paying bills, and distributing assets. However, such estates almost invariably have the extra and somewhat costly problem of paying premiums for performance bonds issued by an insurance company. This expense can sometimes be avoided by having people post personal bonds. A personal bond is one provided by a person or persons who own adequate real or personal property. Such people join the administrator to guarantee his or her honest and competent performance in completing the administration duties. Courts generally accept bonds from insurance companies more readily than personal bonds. Bonds are not cancelled until the estate is settled to the satisfaction of the court at a formal closing. Costs for surety bonds are paid by the estate.

Courts set bond amounts, and there is a rule in some provinces that those provided by insurance companies are to be for amounts equal to one and a half times the value of the deceased's personal property. Personal bond amounts may be as high as twice the value. Insurance premiums are payable annually until the estate is settled. Performance bonds are seldom required when there is a valid will that can be probated, except when the executor is a non-resident of the province or territory. While court requirements vary between jurisdictions, trust companies are generally not required to provide bonds when they are appointed to administer estates.

Intestate succession laws distribute estates primarily on the basis of blood relationships. Statutes vary in each jurisdiction and other applicable laws can complicate the distribution of assets. When a person dies with neither a will nor any traceable relatives, the residue of their estate, after taxes, reverts to the government's coffers (see chart page 61).

Not making a valid will leaves a mess for someone else to clean up. In summary, if you die intestate:

1. ***Your estate will be distributed according to succession laws.*** Not only can the distribution be far from what you would have wanted, it can also get tied up in costly, lengthy legal tangles and the law may prevent payments for a year or more.

2. ***The court might appoint someone you would not have chosen to administer your estate.***

3. ***If you have not made legal provisions for a guardian for minor children, the court will appoint one, again, likely not the person you would have chose***n.

4. ***You will have missed the opportunity to do estate tax planning, which is one of the benefits of making a will.*** Money from your estate may needlessly go to pay taxes that would have otherwise been avoided.

CONTESTING A DECEASED'S WILL
What can a dependant(s) do where a testator dies without having made adequate provision in his/ her will for the proper maintainance and support for dependant(s)?

Provinces and territories have enacted testators' family maintenance; family maintenance; matrimonial property, and other legislation designed to protect dependants from misuse and undue hardships. Statutes state procedures to be followed to challenge wills of deceased persons,

The following chart gives a brief picture of intestate succession laws in the provinces and territories. Any questions it prompts can best be answered by referring to the applicable statutes, particularly with regard to safeguarding inheritances to underage children.

DISTRIBUTION OF ESTATES ACCORDING TO PROVINCIAL AND TERRITORIAL INTERSTATE LAWS (SUBJECT TO CHANGES AND INTERPRETATIONS)

JURISDICTION	SPOUSE, NO CHILDREN	CHILD OR CHILDREN, NO SPOUSE	SPOUSE AND ONE CHILD	SPOUSE AND MORE THAN ONE CHILD	NO SPOUSE AND NO CHILDREN
Alberta	All to spouse	All to children; if any deceased, to their issue	1st $40,000 to spouse and rest split 50/50	1st $40,000 to spouse plus 1/3 of rest, 2/3 to children	ALL TO NEXT OF KIN In the following order: 1st to living parent/ parents 2nd to brothers/sisters but if any deceased, their descendants receive their parent's share 3rd if parents, brothers and sisters have not survived, to nieces/nephews 4th to traceable next of kin 5th to the government if no next of kin is found.
British Columbia	All to spouse	All to children; if any deceased, to their issue	1st $65,000 to spouse and rest split 50/50	1st $65,000 to spouse plus 1/3 of rest, 2/3 to children	
Manitoba	All to spouse	All to children; if any deceased, to their issue	All to spouse if child/children are deceased's issue, otherwise spouse's and children's shares are different		
New Brunswick	All to spouse	All to children; if any deceased, to their issue	Spouse gets marital property and rest split 50/50	Spouse gets marital property plus 1/3 of rest, 2/3 to children	
Newfoundland	All to spouse	All to children; if any deceased, to their issue	Split 50/50	1/3 to spouse and 2/3 to children	
Northwest Territories	All to spouse	All to children; if any deceased, to their issue	1st $50,000 to spouse and rest split 50/50	1st $50,000 to spouse plus 1/3 of rest, 2/3 to children	
Nova Scotia	All to spouse	All to children; if any deceased, to their issue	1st $50,000 to spouse and rest split 50/50	1st $50,000 to spouse plus 1/3 of rest, 2/3 to children	
Nunavut*	All to spouse	All to children; if any deceased, to their issue	1st $50,000 to spouse and rest split 50/50	1st $50,000 to spouse plus 1/3 of rest, 2/3 to children	
Ontario	All to spouse	All to children; if any deceased, to their issue	1st $200,000 to spouse and rest split 50/50	1st $200,000 to spouse plus 1/3 of rest and 2/3 to children	
Prince Edward Island	All to spouse	All to children; if any deceased, to their issue	Split 50/50	1/3 to spouse 2/3 to children	
Quebec	All to spouse but relatives can share	All to children; if any deceased, to their issue	1/3 to spouse and 2/3 to child	1/3 to spouse and 2/3 to children	
Saskatchewan	All to spouse	All to children; if any deceased, to their issue	1st $100,000 to spouse plus 1/3 of rest, 2/3 to child	1st $100,000 to spouse plus 1/3 of rest, 2/3 to children	
Yukon Territory	All to spouse	All to children; if any deceased, to their issue	Split 50/50	1/3 to spouse and 2/3 to children	

* The new territory, April, 1999, which will initially use laws of the Northwest Territories.

Note: The above presentation is intended to give a general picture of the persons to whom the estate of an intestate may have to be distributed in each province and territory. Applicable statutes in each jurisdiction, such as child and family acts, Quebec Civil Code; Marital Property acts, Family Law acts, Intestate and Succession acts need to be examined as they can be at variance with this presentation. Items such as living common law, living in adultery, divorced, adopted, a dependant of the deceased, can change distribution formulas.

regardless of whether or not the wills have already been probated in common form. A deceased testator's will can for reason be contested by any person having an interest in the estate by applying to the courts to have the will changed, or declared invalid. Spouses and dependants can be protected from a parent or the other spouse ignoring responsibility for the care and maintenance of his (or her) dependants. If a deceased spouse's will proposes to distribute his (or her) assets without adequately providing for dependants, the will should be contested. Then the courts can order appropriate changes. Such orders could require the executor to cease making any distribution of estate assets other than those approved by a judge, and paying the bills.

Should a deceased testator's last will be declared invalid, then intestate succession distribution laws would apply.

SMALL ESTATES WHERE THERE IS A WILL

It may be unnecessary to probate when assets are of limited value. The executor named in the will can usually use the deceased's funds to pay the bills and make distributions without the expense of probating the will. For instance, when there is a will but the executor decides not to probate it, chartered banks may legally allow the release of up to $25,000 of the deceased's funds. This can generally be done at the branch manager's discretion if the deceased was a well-known customer and if the executor and beneficiaries are also known and considered responsible for the amount involved. The deposit may well be the only significant asset in the estate. Documentation a bank would generally require in such a circumstance is:

1. *An authenticated copy of the will and codicil(s), if any;*

2. *An authenticated copy of the death certificate, act of death certificate, or*

funeral director's statement of death;

3. *A bond of indemnity (the bank's document which indemnifies it from incurring any loss as a result of releasing the funds to the executor named in the will).* The document has to be signed by one or more persons who the bank is satisfied can pay the amount of any claims that may be made. The executor is invariably a surety;

4. *The bank may also require a sworn declaration of transmission.*

Motor vehicle registries in Nova Scotia can transfer ownership of vehicles when the net value of the deceased's assets does not exceed $50,000. The executor has to show the original will, provide proof of death, and sign the transfer form. Similar treatment can be expected in other jurisdictions.

An executor can arrange for the funeral, take control of and protect assets, and even pay bills—but in doing so he is not personally protected from liability claims made against him. Such a problem might arise, for example, if beneficiaries under a will felt that the executor had wasted or misspent the deceased's money. In this case the beneficiaries could file a legal claim against the executor in his personal capacity in the hope of recovering perceived losses.

In the case of small estates where there is no will, it is often not necessary that a personal representative apply to the court for letters of administration. Banks do not usually require letters of administration when account balances are less than $25,000 though they will probably require the following documents:

1. *The bank's sworn declaration of transmission.*

2. *An authenticated proof of death.*

3. *A bond of indemnity.* Again, the people signing the bank's agreement must be credit-worthy and considered by the bank to be financially responsible for the amount released from the deceased's accounts.

4. *The bank may also require to be provided with a sworn declaration made by the people interested in the estate, in which relevant details are included.*

When these documents have been provided, the personal representative of the deceased, acting as the administrator, can expect the bank to release funds to pay funeral costs and immediate expenses. In some instances the funds are released upon receiving mere proof of death.

When banks hold properties in excess of $25,000 solely in the name of a deceased depositor, they may need authenticated letters of administration (with or without will annexed) before they will release more than $25,000.

Registries of motor vehicles in Nova Scotia can transfer ownership of vehicles when the net value of the intestate's assets do not exceed $50,000 if they are provided with a proof of death and a statutory declaration (exhibit no. 39).

XIV

POWERS OF ATTORNEY AND GUARDIANSHIPS

While many of us may have made our wills and regularly update them, very few people have arranged for someone to handle their affairs should they become incapacitated. Accidents happen, and not always to somebody else. A sudden illness or accident can make it impossible for us to pay our bills and take care of our belongings. If we become incapacitated, and medical opinion is the condition may last for some time, unless we have given someone a power of attorney to act for us, all of our affairs are indefinitely put on hold. When this happens, the only way someone else can legally look after our property is if they are appointed our legal guardian by a court. That someone is usually a next of kin who may or may not be the person we would have chosen to take charge of our estate. The simple way to avoid this problem is to give a person or persons power of attorney over our affairs.

A Power of Attorney is a legal document that authorizes the person you appoint as your attorney to transact business in your name as long as you are alive. (Note that "attorney" does not necessarily mean "lawyer.") A General Power of Attorney is a powerful document and should only be given to someone you fully trust, usually a family member. It can be given to more than one person and can be revoked at any time. The wording used in powers of attorney can limit the scope of what the attorney can do in your name, and even the circumstances under which the power comes into effect. As long as you remain mentally competent and alert, the attorney has authority to transact business for you under a general power of attorney. That authority ceases, however, in the event that you become mentally incapacitated and unable to look after your affairs yourself, unless the document contains a clause making it a continuing or enduring power of attorney.

While each province has its own laws relating to powers of attorney, they are all similar. The document entitled Power of Attorney to Transfer Securities (exhibit no. 15) is an example of an appointment that gives the appointee only the authorization to do something specific: transfer registration of a security.

I have an elderly relative who gave me his enduring power of attorney when he had to move into a nursing home several years ago. He subsequently became mentally and physically incapacitated and unable to look after his affairs. His elderly wife continues to live in their original residence and the couple had no children and no next of kin to carry on the business. The relative was the sole owner of several parcels of land but since his decline his land holdings had generated little revenue and accumulated property tax costs. It therefore was of benefit to him that the enduring power of attorney enabled me to sell the properties. (It was necessary to have the Power of Attorney document recorded in the county's registry of deeds to permanently have on record that I had legal authority to sell and give good title to purchasers.) An example of the type of document necessary in this case is an Enduring Power of Attorney (exhibit no. 40).

A woman in her sixties had a severe stroke several years ago. She suffered brain damage and lost the ability to communicate except for making a few hand signals and sounds. Fortunately, some years prior to her illness she had given an enduring power of attorney to her daughter, which made it easy for her to look after her mother's affairs and personal care. But for this enduring power of attorney it would have been necessary for the daughter to apply to the courts to be appointed her mother's guardian. That appointment would have incurred high legal and bonding expenses, as well as the time and expense of providing annual reports to the Supreme Court of Nova Scotia. Applying for guardianship involves considerably more expense and work than probating a will—even for a family member. Affidavits have to be obtained from two or more medical practitioners verifying that the person is truly incapacitated; financial listings of all assets and liabilities have to be attested and provided to the court annually (sometimes more regularly); and the guardian has to be bonded for amounts which can range from 125 to 200 per cent of the value of total assets. The bond cannot be cancelled without court approval, preceded by a final accounting of it. If the incapacitated person's health recovers sufficiently, guardianship can cease; otherwise it ends upon death, and then all assets are turned over to the executor appointed in the person's will. If the guardian dies, resigns, or cannot continue

to act, someone has to apply to the court to be appointed the new guardian. Statutes requiring guardians to provide a surety bond generally state that it can be provided by one or more individuals. Individuals offering to sign bonds in support of an application for someone to be appointed a guardian are required to provide proof to the court that they have sufficient assets to be able to honour their undertaking as sureties. Except where the value of the incompetent person's assets is small, it can be very difficult to find someone who is willing to sign a surety bond. The alternative is to obtain the bond from an insurance company.

A fourteen-page booklet prepared in 1996 by the Public Guardian and Trustee (595 Bay Street, Toronto, Ontario, M5G 2M6) entitled "Powers of Attorney" contains detailed information about power of attorney forms. It has definitions and a good summary of the items to be considered when appointing someone to be an attorney. The booklet also contains two forms acceptable in Ontario for appointing attorneys, entitled Continuing Power of Attorney for Property (exhibit no. 41) and Power of Attorney for Personal Care (exhibit no. 42).

In Ontario a person appointed by a continuing power of attorney for property is entitled to compensation at the same rate allowed to appointed property guardians. The rates are 2.5 per cent of the money received and paid out, plus two-fifths of one per cent of the average annual value of assets. You must be at least eighteen years of age and mentally capable to make a valid continuing power of attorney for property. The person(s) you appoint can make decisions about your property and manage your financial affairs, regardless of whether or not you are mentally incapable of doing so yourself. The document does not, however, allow your attorney to make decisions about your personal care.

The Power of Attorney for Personal Care form meets the legal requirements of Ontario's *Substitute Decisions Act*. It is understood to be a "living will."

This kind of power of attorney gives the appointed person(s) authority concerning your health care in the event that you become mentally incapacitated. The attorney is responsible for making decisions about your care. For instance, he or she can decide whether you will continue to live in your present residence or be moved elsewhere. The attorney also has the authority to make decisions about any category of personal care which you are incapable of judging for yourself, including the right to refuse medical treatment. However, the document does not allow your attorney to make decisions about your property or finances. You cannot appoint someone as your attorney for personal care unless you have reached the age of sixteen, and the person you appoint must be at least eighteen. Some people are not allowed to be an attorney for personal care if they charge for their services, unless they are also the spouse, partner, or relative of the person in question. It is possible to appoint more than one attorney to have them either make decisions together, or act separately. Also, substitute attorneys can be appointed.

Both Power of Attorney documents, when completed, should be kept in a safe place where the appointed attorneys, family members, a solicitor, or friends can quickly locate them. The booklet also contains a card that one can carry on their person which states whom he or she has appointed as attorney.

You can revoke a power of attorney you have given at any time by notifying the person(s) you appointed. A written notice of the revocation must be provided to the person(s) and also given to any provincial or other registry office where the document has been recorded, as well as any institution with whom your attorney(s) may have transacted business in your name. If possible, you should recover the appointment document.

GUARDIANSHIP/TUTORSHIP

When a person becomes mentally incompetent, and has not given anyone a continuing or enduring power of attorney, the process is somewhat similar to that of an intestacy. A spouse, next of kin, or relative applies to the court to be appointed guardian of the incompetent person's estate. Courts place strict duties and requirements on guardians: They must immediately prepare an inventory of assets and file it with the courts, they must safeguard all properties, maintain investments in qualified funds, and provide accounting reports to the court annually or whenever directed. A guardian has the authority to consent to medical treatment or other procedures to be administered to the incompetent person, and to choose the hospitals, institutions, or residences in which the person is to be treated, housed, and maintained. Statutes dictate how guardianship compensation is to be calculated.

Before the appointed guardian can commence his or her duties, he or she must provide the court with a performance guarantee, generally called a bond. These are issued either by an insurance company or given by one or more sureties, similar to the requirements expected of administrators of intestacies. The bond amount varies and can range from the inventory's value to double the inventory's amount. Again, bonds are usually obtained from an insurance company due to the difficulties of finding individuals willing to give personal guarantees to the court until the guardianship terminates. Only after the guardian's final accounting report has been received and accepted by the court are the guarantees terminated.

In the event that funds under the guardians' control have been misused, the sureties can be required to pay money to the court. In one instance where assets were $120,000, the insurance company's yearly premium for a $165,000 bond was $440, and legal costs incurred to obtain the appointment were $1,025. Both expenses were paid from the assets of the incompetent person, as was the guardian's compensation.

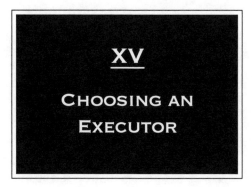

An executor, executrix, or liquidator is the person or trust company you appoint to carry out your wishes when you die. In your will you can appoint one or more executors; to name two is quite common, and sometimes three are named. To have more than two people administer your estate, however, can be cumbersome and unnecessarily time-consuming for them and your heirs. Alternate executors should always be appointed in the event that those who were first appointed cannot or will not act. It is advantageous to have an executor who resides in the same province as you, because he will be subject to the laws of your province or territory and under the jurisdiction of their courts; otherwise he or she may be required to post a performance bond.

A will made in accordance with the laws of the jurisdiction in which you are living does not become invalid if you change residence to another jurisdiction. A valid will made in Nova Scotia can be probated anywhere in Canada as well in some other countries.

It is very important to keep in mind that the executor you appoint will have the authority to act on and take control of everything from the moment you die. This includes making funeral arrangements, gathering all assets and protecting them, paying debts and taxes, and distributing property according to the will. When there are underage children the executor must see that their inheritance is protected and that funds are placed in trusts for them.

Probate courts have no jurisdiction over property located outside of their province or territory. Once probate of a will has been granted in the deceased's province or territory of residency, it is necessary to apply to have the document resealed by the court in any other province or territory where the deceased had property. When a court places its seal on the document, the appointments made in other jurisdictions are legally recognized and the executor can administer estate assets located within that court's jurisdiction. Wills probated in the United Kingdom, the British Commonwealth, and some other countries can be resealed in Canada. The process also works in reverse. A somewhat unusual case I once came across was that of a testator residing in the United Kingdom who also had assets in Nova Scotia. The complication in his will was the appointment of two executors residing in the United Kingdom to administer his assets there and a Nova Scotia resident to be his "foreign trustee" to administer assets in Canada. When he died, the two United Kingdom executors applied for and were granted administration only of his assets located in Britain. The Nova Scotia registrar of probate initially chose not to reseal the will probated in London, but when the executor had the matter referred to the Supreme Court of Nova Scotia, the documents were resealed. The executor then sold and disposed of the assets in Nova Scotia as directed by the will.

Choosing your executor should be a carefully thought-out decision. Ideally, the person will be somewhat knowledgeable about estates, possess some accounting skills, be well organized, a good communicator, honest, responsible, assertive, and reliable. The appointment should never be made with the idea of bestowing an honour. An executor's responsibilities end when the estate is settled, yet decisions made during the administration process can have a significant impact (either positive or negative) on the deceased's heirs for years to come. An incompetent executor can easily cause inexcusable and costly delays in safeguarding the testator's properties and carrying out the instructions in his or her will. It is also difficult, time-consuming, and somewhat costly to have an executor's appointment revoked.

Minors are not eligible to be appointed executors. When a will names a minor to be the sole executor, the administration of an estate may be granted to a minor's guardian until he becomes of age.

The first thing an executor must do is take control of all the deceased's assets. He or she is responsible for their safekeeping and must protect them. He or she must check that properties are adequately insured, all assets are located, insurance benefits collected, all heirs identified, and he or she must clearly understand the instructions in the will. You can make things a lot easier for your executor if you make a list of your investments, bank accounts, safety deposit box contents, real estate holdings, and any loans and private investments you may have with individuals or businesses. Also helpful is a dated list of loans and mortgages owed, and a note stating where your last will and safety deposit box key can be found. If, after making the will, you decide you want to give certain personal effects of limited monetary value to specific people, the simplest thing to do is to make a memorandum. Address the memo to the executor, and leave it in a sealed envelope where it will easily be found.

A testator can state in his or her will the rate or commission fee to be paid to the executor. When probate has been completed, the court may or may not agree with the amount and may change it if it appears unreasonable in relation to the work done by the executor.

Chapter 10 of this book summarizes the steps Mary Fraser took to administer and settle her husband's estate. While no two estates are the same, there is a similarity in the steps and requirements to settle all but unusually complex estates. The larger the estate, the larger the risk of legal complications. A trend popular at the moment is to distribute one's assets while one is still living. When probate has been granted to an executor and he or she dies before completing the work, in many jurisdictions his or her executor will automatically become executor of both estates. However, the new executor can renounce executorship of the former estate if they don't want that responsibility. It is possible for there to be a succession of executors with the chain finally broken by an intestacy. Prince Edward Island laws do not allow this procedure and require that someone apply to the probate court to be appointed administrator to complete administration of the estate. The new executor can apply for the appointment.

What can be done when an executor or appointed administrator fails, procrastinates, misuses assets, or is just plain negligent in fulfilling his duties and responsibilities? What action can the beneficiaries and heirs take? What steps can be taken to have appointments of administrators and executors revoked?

These are tough questions but worth asking, since situations do develop where heirs and beneficiaries have reason to want the appointed executor removed. The first step is to gather all documentation and details of the appointee's wrongful acts, incompetence, inertia, etc., and take the information to the clerk or registrar of the court involved for guidance on how to proceed. Otherwise, seek advice from a lawyer, who will explain how to obtain a citation ordering a hearing. If the court is satisfied that the complaints are justified, it may remove the executor and appoint an administrator provided that the executor:

- has been negligent, tardy, and wasteful in settling the estate, or
- has failed to obey a court order, or
- lives outside the jurisdiction of the court, or
- has neglected to settle or administer the estate, or
- has failed to comply with an order to pay into a chartered bank or other approved financial institution estate money that has come into his or her hands.

The following chart summarizes the more common elements an executor must deal with. Note that in some jurisdictions the sequence may vary.

DUTIES OF AN EXECUTOR

Receive Notification of Death	
Make Funeral Arrangements	
❏ Meet with family members to study and discuss the will.	❏ Select a lawyer or notary for the estate to use as and when required.
Assemble Inventory and Take Custody of Assets	
❏ Search for assets. List contents of all safety deposit boxes.	❏ Examine employment contracts and deferred compensation agreements.
❏ Ensure adequate coverage on real estate and personal property insurance policies and get endorsements with any loss payable to estate.	❏ File claims for life insurance, pension, and other death benefits.
❏ Prepare list of assets with estimated values and list of known debts.	❏ Inspect all real estate. Study any leases and mortgages.
Review Financial Records	
❏ Review and study business interests, partnerships and operating companies that may be part of estate.	❏ Study income tax returns for prior years to gather data of financial history.
Arrange for Probate of Will	
❏ Receive court authority to act for estate.	❏ Notify banks, brokers, other asset holders.
❏ Arrange for bond if required by court.	❏ Arrange public notice to creditors and others.
	❏ Open estate banking account.
Administer the Estate, Subject to the Provisions of the Will	
❏ Collect all income, receivables, and any monies due.	❏ Estimate cash needed to pay legacies, taxes, debts, and costs to be incurred. Select assets to be liquidated to raise cash.
❏ Examine any claims on the estate for validity and reject those that are unreasonable.	❏ Defend any litigation against the estate.
Ensure Non-Probate Assets are Looked After	
❏ Assets that do not pass under the will, such as life insurance payable to a named beneficiary, must be dealt with when settling an estate.	❏ Clothing and personal effects.
Prepare all Tax Returns	
Income Taxes	
❏ Calculate taxable gains (or losses) arising on death.	❏ File returns for any assets located in foreign countries, where required.
❏ File final tax return for deceased.	
❏ Obtain final tax clearance certificate prior to distribution.	
❏ File tax returns for estate during period of administration.	
❏ Obtain waivers, releases, and clearance certificates as necessary for transfer of assets.	
Distribute the Estate, Close it	
❏ Obtain releases from beneficiaries.	❏ Distribute residue as directed in the will.
❏ Account for all assets, income, and disbursements.	❏ Retain all original documents, tax clearances, receipts, and releases indefinitely.
❏ Obtain court discharge if necessary or desired.	❏ Arrange for any continuing trusts.

When an executor is removed, he or she will be required to submit a final accounting of the estate to the court. The court will review the work he or she has done. Beneficiaries, heirs, and interested parties will also have the opportunity to review it at that time. In the event beneficiaries suffer losses or damages caused by an executor or trustee acting in bad faith, the injured parties may have grounds to take legal action against the executor personally to recover their losses.

Many national trust companies, investment dealers, financial advisors, and others have free pamphlets listing the duties of an executor. The following is a list of the prime duties and responsibilities of an executor.

One of the last steps of an executor, according to the accompanying chart is to "obtain court discharge if necessary or desired." In other words, the executor should have a formal closing or, if this is not required by the court, beneficiaries, or other parties with an interest in the estate, an informal one. When probate is granted, the court may direct the executor to file a final account of his or her administration of the estate to formally close it. When the executor has a formal closing and his or her report is accepted, the court issues a final decree order or other acknowledgement of the fact that the court has received and passed the administrator's accounts. Mary Fraser followed this procedure and obtained a final decree order, which is the normal requirement in Nova Scotia. While a decree does not completely release the executor from the responsibility of administering an estate, it does put on permanent record that the court has examined and accepted his or her stewardship report. In addition, it records that the executor gave ample time for anyone interested in the estate to come forth and present claims against it, and that his or her commission fee, legacies, gifts, debt payments, and residual distributions were approved by the court.

An informal closing of an estate takes place when the executor does not present a final accounting of his or her executorship to a court. In these instances there are usually few residual beneficiaries, and the executor is often a close relative or friend of the deceased and family. After all bequests, debts, bills, and taxes have been paid, and the executor is confident that whatever is left is available for distribution to residual beneficiaries, he or she can reasonably pay out the money and close the estate, unless the court or applicable statutes order otherwise. However, it is strongly recommended that the executor obtain documents from all residual beneficiaries approving his or her final accounts and releasing him or her from future claims by them. Had Mary Fraser chosen not to have a formal closing, she might have used a document similar to the release (exhibit no. 43).

XVI
MINIMIZING ESTATE PROBATE FEES

There are ways of reducing estate fees or the cost of having a will probated. (Provincial governments are continually trying to find ways to increase revenues, and probate fees have been one of their many targets, probably because there are presently no succession taxes in Canada.) Trying to minimize the total value of estate assets is always worth the time and effort involved because probate fees are based on inventory valuations. (A fee is also charged when an estate is formally closed.) In some jurisdictions real estate is not included for the purpose of calculating probate fees; in others it is. There are several items you might want to consider in deciding what will or will not be part of your estate:

• RRSP/RRIF accounts naming your spouse as beneficiary. In the event of your death, the account is transferred directly to your spouse; thus it does not become part of your estate's inventory. RRSP/RRIF transfers to spouses have no income tax consequences.

• Real estate holdings. When the owners are registered as "joint tenants" and not "tenants in common," the ownership passes to the surviving person(s) without becoming an estate asset and thus part of the estate's inventory. The income tax implications caused by registering assets (other than the family residence and bank accounts) in joint names should be carefully researched before this is done. When ownership of other real estate or any asset is transferred into joint ownership ("joint" implying right of survivorship) Revenue Canada deems one half to have been sold; this could create taxable capital gains. Joint survivorship rules applicable in other provinces are not applicable in Quebec.

• With mortgaged real estate, deduct the amount of outstanding mortgages from the inventory valuation, recording only the net value of the property.

• By placing bank accounts, investments, vehicles, boats, and such items in two or more names in common, ownership automatically passes to the survivor(s) when one of the registered owners dies. Thereby the assets do not become part the deceased's estate. However, all parties must have full trust in one another, because each joint owner has full authority over the assets, except matrimonial property. Again, the income tax implications should be carefully researched in advance.

- Real and personal property located outside the province or territory where the will is probated or resealed should not be included in the list of the deceased's assets presented to the court. Each province and territory, almost without exception, collects probate fees based only on the value of assets located inside their jurisdiction.
- Set up a living trust which can hold assets so they do not fall into your estate when you die. Living trusts are not appropriate for everyone, and the implications of establishing them require careful consideration of tax and legal risks. Trusts can be an effective tax-planning vehicle, tailored to suit many needs, and allow access to income and capital as long as you are alive, but setting one up requires a lot of planning with tax and legal advisors.

Insolvent Estates

Personal bankruptcies are not uncommon and estates are sometimes insolvent. An estate is insolvent if the value of assets is not large enough to pay outstanding debts, claims, and testamentary expenses. What can happen in such a situation is that the executor named in the will or a personal representative of the deceased applies to the court for an insolvency order declaring the estate to be insolvent. The application is supported by a list of claims and expenses which will be chargeable to the estate showing that the total estimated value of the estate is less than the claims and expenses. The question then becomes, what are the priorities for payment from estate funds? Ignoring variances in provincial statutes, legal priorities basically are:

PROBATE FEES

A schedule of Canadian probate fees in effect at the end of 1997

PROVINCE OR TERRITORY	FEES
Alberta	Starting at $25 for the first $10,000, then graduated increases take the fee up to $6,000 for estates over $1,000,000.
British Columbia	No charge under $10,000; $200 for next $15,000; then $6 per $1,0000 up to $50,000 plus $50; $14 per $1,000 thereafter less $350. No maximum.
Manitoba	$25 on first $5,000 and then $6 per $1,000. No maximum.
Newfoundland	$50 on first $1,000 plus $10 fee; and then $4 per $1,000. No maximum.
Northwest Territories	$8 on first $500; $15 for $501 to $1,000; then $3 per $1,000. No maximum.
New Brunswick	$5 per $1,000. No maximum.
Nova Scotia	$75 for first $10,000, then fee graduated up to $800 for estates of $200,000; then $5 per $1,000. No maximum.
Ontario	$5 per $1,000 on first $50,000; then $15 per $1,000. No maximum.
Prince Edward Island	$50 for first $10,000, then graduated up to $400 for estates of $100,000; then $4 per $1,000. No maximum.
Quebec	Notarial wills are not probated. For other forms of will the fee is $45.
Saskatchewan	$7 per $1,000, no maximum.
Yukon Territory	No fee for estates under $10,000; $140 for $10,001 to $25,000; and then $6 per $1,000. No maximum.

1. Funeral expenses.

2. While Revenue Canada is first in line for any outstanding income taxes, as might be expected, in practice they recognize the deceased is entitled to a dignified burial and allow the expense to be paid. Also they generally can be expected to allow reasonable funeral, gravestone, and expenses to settle the estate to be paid, including executor or administrator fees.

3. Costs of necessary medical care during the last illness before death. When remaining assets are insufficient to cover these items in full, they are settled in proportion to their claims. Each receives an equal percentage of the amount claimed.

4. If money is left after the above claims have been paid, it goes to pay any amounts owing to employees as at date of death, possibly limited to amounts unpaid for one year. Again, if payments cannot be made in full, claims are settled PRO RATA.

5. Remaining funds are distributed to unsecured creditors PRO RATA.

6. Debts secured by mortgages and judgements registered on real estate or personal property, such as boats and vehicles, may not be affected by an estate's insolvency. Holders of mortgages and judgements which have been registered as charges against real and personal assets are classified as secured creditors who can foreclose on and sell the security to collect the amounts owing to them. If, when the security is sold, the proceeds do not pay off the debt against it, the "secured" creditor becomes an unsecured creditor for the difference. Whenever secured creditors realize more from the sale of the security they held than was owing, the surplus is paid to the executor or administrator for the benefit of other creditors.

EXHIBITS

Exhibits and the pages on which they are introduced

EXHIBIT 1, PAGE 1: FUNERAL DIRECTOR'S WORKING FILE

SERVICE FOR:

Fraser, James Robert

Date: May 24, 1997

Family Contacts: Mary Fraser, Christopher Fraser   Relationship: Wife & Son
Address: 937 Crichton Avenue, Dartmouth   Phone: 469-5662

NAME OF DECEASED	1. Surname of deceased (print or type) **FRASER**	S.I.N. **414-712-216**
	All given names in full (print or type) **JAMES ROBERT**	2. Sex **M**
		HOSPITAL: Phoned
PLACE OF DEATH	3. Name of hospital or institution (otherwise give exact location where death occurred) **DARTMOUTH GENERAL HOSPITAL** Date of Death **MAY 24**	
	City, town or other place (by name) **DARTMOUTH** Postal Code Inside municipal limits? (State Yes or No)	
USUAL RESIDENCE	4. Complete street address. If rural give exact location (Not Post Office or Rural Route Address) **937 CRICHTON AVE.**	**RELEASED:** May 24
	City, town or other place (by name) **DARTMOUTH** Postal Code **B3A4T7** Inside municipal limits? (State Yes or No) **Yes** Province (or Country) **N.S.**	**TIME:** 12.50 PM
MARITAL STATUS	5. Single, married, widowed, or divorced (Specify) **Married** 6. If married, widowed, or divorced, give full name of husband or full maiden name of wife **MARY ANN JOHNSTON**	**AUTOPSY:** No
OCCUPATION	7. Kind of work done during most of working life **Sales** 8. Kind of business or industry in which worked **Telephone company**	**PERSONAL EFFECTS:** To son
BIRTHDATE	9. Month (by name), day, year of birth **FEB. 21, 1934** 10. Age (years) **62** (Months) (Days) If under 1 year (Hours) (Minutes) If under 1 day	
BIRTHPLACE	11. City or place Province (or Country) of birth **STELLARTON, N.S.** 12. Native Indian? Yes ☐ No ☐ If "yes" state name of band	
FATHER	13. Surname and given names of father (print or type) **FRASER, DUNCAN ROSS** 14. Birthplace – City or place, Province (or Country) **MONTREAL, QUEBEC**	**COMMENTS:**
MOTHER	15. Maiden surname and given names of mother (print or type) **WHALEN, MARGARET JANE** 16. Birthplace – City or place, Province (or Country) **FREDERICTON, N.B.**	
INFORMANT	17. Signature of informant **X Mary A. Fraser** 18. Relationship to deceased **Wife**	
	19. Address of informant **937 Crichton Avenue, Dartmouth** 20. Date signed – Month, Day, Year **May 24, 1996**	
DISPOSITION	21. Burial, cremation or other disposition (specify) **Burial** 22. Date of burial or disposition (Month, Day Year)	
	23. Name and address of cemetery, crematorium or place of disposition **Sackville Cemetery**	
DOCTOR	24. Name and address **Dr. Ruben Offman, Woodside Medical Clinic**	
DATE	25. Date of funeral service **May 26** 26. Time **2:30 P.M.**	
PLACE	27. Place of funeral service **Woodside United Church** 28. Religion **United**	
OFFICIATING	29. Name of pastor, clergy or person in charge of funeral service **Rev. Harry Cleves** Notified ☐ 30. Phone Number(s) **454-6669**	
	31. Send car to **937 C.** Honourarium direct from family: No ☐ Yes ☐ "No" cheque for $ **100** – **Minister** ☐ ☑ Committal service to be held: In chapel/church ☐ At crematory/cemetery ☑	
MUSIC	32. Name of organist **JOSEPHINE HUNT** Notified ☑ 33. Hymn(s) to be sung by congregation **Abide With Me The Hills & Glens –** $50 to organist	
	34. Name of soloist Notified ☐ 35. Solo(s) to be sung by soloist	
FAMILY CAR	36. Yes ☑ No ☐ If "Yes" number of cars to call at what address **1 car to 937 Crichton Avenue** 37. Time **2.15 PM**	
FAMILY SEATING	38. Family to sit in Chapel ☐ Family room ☐ Specify additional seating arrangements	
VIEWING	39. Yes ☑ No ☐ If "Yes" give specific viewing procedure **Closed Casket** Date: **May 25** Time: **7:00 – 9:00 PM** Place: **Funeral Home**	
PRAYERS	40. Yes ☐ No ☑ Date: Time: Place:	
CASKET	41. Open ☐ Closed ☑ Before service ☑ During service ☑ After service ☑	
EXTRA PARTICIPANTS	42. Legion ☐ Fraternal ☐ Other ☐	
FLAG	43. Maple Leaf ☐ Union Jack ☐ Other ☐	

EXHIBIT 1, PAGE 2: FUNERAL DIRECTOR'S WORKING FILE

DEATH CERTIFICATE RELEASED TO			*Mary A. Fraser*			Date *May 28/97*
CERTIFICATES	How many *6*	Mail ☐	Deliver ☒	Name & address of party to receive certificates		Ordered ☐
PREPARATION	Embalming Yes ☒ No ☐	Approx. Weight & Height *190 lbs 5'8"*		Cosmetics – Give special inst.	Clothing None ☐	Coming ☒ Here ☐
	Hairdresser Yes ☐ No ☒	Notified ☐		Hairstyle – Give specific instructions		Ready for viewing *May 24 – 4 PM*
JEWELERY	Give list of jewelery and specific instructions for disposal *Wedding ring to Mary Fraser or son*					
FLOWERS YES or NO	*Family roses on casket*					
MEMORIAL	Register ☒ Service Cards ☒ Quantity *125* Acknowledgement Cards ☒ *100*					
OBITUARIES	Paper ☒ Others– *Family will provide*					
FAMILY NAMES	*Children – Elizabeth Jane married Charles Wilson* *– Christopher Robert* *Grandchildren – Joanne Wilson* *– Stanley Wilson*					
FRATERNAL ORGANIZATIONS WAR RECORD						
OTHER INFORMATION						
BEARERS	Active Bearers? Yes ☐ No ☐ If "Yes" specify transportation arrangements					
	Honourary Bearers? Yes ☒ No ☐ If "Yes" specify transportation arrangements *Christopher will give us names and phone numbers of 4 men*					
CEMETERY INFORMATION	Lot Description *Lot to be purchased in Sackville Cemetery* New grave ☐ Reserve required ☐ Extra depth ☐					
	Grave previously purchased? ☐ Lot description: Year of purchase:					
CASKET	To be lowered at cemetery? Yes ☒ No ☐					
DISBURSEMENT OF FLOWERS	*To Senior Citizens Home*					
CREMATED REMAINS	Family to receive Yes ☐ No ☐	To be interred at		Family present? Yes ☐ No ☐	Date:	Time:
TEA / RECEPTION	To be announced by Clergy? Yes ☒ No ☐ Other –					
	Address for Tea / Reception – *Woodside United Church basement hall*					
	Will family meet friends at conclusion of service? Yes ☒ No ☐ Where –					

EXHIBIT 1, PAGE 3: FUNERAL DIRECTOR'S WORKING FILE

CASKET	Give complete description including manufacturer or agent *Metro Basic J.P. Embossed Gray Cloth* Ordered ☐
URN	

SHIPPING	Name of funeral director shipped to/from (State which)	Phone number
	Address	Notified ☐
	Name of Carrier, Flight No., Train No. etc.	Phone number	Place, date & time of departure
	Place, date & time of arrival	—Coroners certificate attached ☐

		PRICE	
Professional services *documents funeral stationary guest book, register, proof of death certificates*		1500	—
Care and preparation of deceased *embalming*		400	—
Facilities and funeral home quipment *for reception, May 25*		400	
Automotive equipment *Hospital to Home, to church to cemetery and family car on funeral day*		575	—
Other: *Honouriums – Minister*		100	—
– Organist		50	—
Casket		1360	—
Misc. charges *Opening & closing grave & box*		400	—
Family flowers		75	
Provincial GST/HST tax calculated on $*4710.*		706	50
	TOTAL $	5566	50

CHECK LIST

Contract Signed	☑	C.P.P. Benefit Explained	☐	Last Post Fund Requirements Explained	☐
Death Reg. Signed	☑	D.V.A. Benefit Explained	☐	Provincial Welfare Requirements Explained	☐
Cremation Consent Signed	☐	Automotive Insurance Benefit Explained	☑	Funeral Home Handouts Given	☑
Identification Signed	☑	W.C.B. Benefit Explained	☐	Parking Explained	☑
Family Shown Around Building	☑	O.A.P. Requirements Explained	☐	Family Given Personal Affects (See Over)	☑
Family Seating Explained	☑	Rental Agreement Signed	☐		

Other Information Still Required: _____

Reason For Family Choosing Our Firm: _____

ADMINISTRATIVE FOLLOW-UP

NEWSPAPER/RADIO	✓	DAY OF INSERTION	DATE TO APPEAR	INSERTED BY	TIME	TAKEN BY
Chronicle Herald	✓	*May 24*	*May 25*	*Kirk Orde*	*3.25 PM*	*Shirley*
Daily News	✓	*May 24*	*May 25*	" "	*3.25* ✓	*Joseph*

Reg. to Doctor/Coroner	☐	Rented Cars Booked	☐
Reg. Picked Up	☐	Flowers Ordered	☑
Burial Permit Picked Up	☑	Memorial Reg. Set Out	☑
Death Certificate Obtained	☑	Memorial Cards Printed	☑
Grave Ordered	☑	Acknowledgement Cards	☑
Clergy Contacted	☑	Temporary Gravemarker	☐
Organist Contacted	☑	Permanent Monument Ordered	☐
Soloist/Choir Contacted	☐	Cremains Interred	☐
Additional Staff Contacted	☐	Clergy Information Prepared	☐
		Clergy Honourarium Prepared	☑
		Organist/Soloist Prepared	☑

Family Comments During Arrangements/
Visitation / Service / Interment:

_____

Statement of Account Prepared/Sent To: *Mary Fraser*

EXHIBIT 1, PAGE 4: FUNERAL DIRECTOR'S WORKING FILE

Articles of importance to be returned to family Yes ☒ No ☐ List _Clothes, wedding ring, watch,_

coins $2.74
_____
Articles received to be given to:

X _Korde_
_____
Witness for receipt of articles

X _CR Fraser_
_____
Articles received   signature

May 24, 1996
_____
Date received

I hereby identify the remains X _Mary A. Fraser_
_____
                               Signature

Wife
_____
Relationship

Korde
_____
Witness for identification

May 24 1996
_____
Date

I hereby received and accept full
responsibility for cremains   X
_____
                               Signature

_____
Relationship

_____
Date

_____
Witness at acceptance of cremains

I hereby instruct the Funeral Director to embalm the remains.   Yes ☒ No ☐

X _Mary A. Fraser_
_____
  Signature

Wife
_____
Relationship

May 24, 1996
_____
Date

I hereby waive my right of identification.

X
_____
  Signature

_____
Relationship

_____
Date

NOTES:

LAST WILL AND TESTAMENT
OF
JAMES ROBERT FRASER

I, JAMES ROBERT FRASER of Dartmouth, in the County of Halifax, Province of Nova Scotia, do make this my last Will and Testament and I revoke all former Wills made by me. ------------

1.   I appoint my wife MARY ANN FRASER to be the executor of my Will; provided that if she predeceases me or if she becomes unable or unwilling to act or continue to act as my executor, I appoint my son CHRISTOPHER ROBERT FRASER and my daughter ELIZABETH JANE WILSON, or the survivor of them to be my executor in her place.--

2.   I declare:

(a) That the term "executor" refers to my executor or executors as the case may be and any reference to my executor in the singular form shall be deemed to include the plural form and words importing any gender shall be deemed to include the other genders.------------------------

(b) That without imposing any trust or legal obligation upon my executor it is my wish and desire that where practicable and possible she honour the terms of any memorandum of division that I may leave at the time of my death relating to distribution of any particular articles of personal possessions and I request my executor and heirs that they distribute such articles pursuant thereto. --------------------

3.   I direct my executor to pay out of the capital of my estate all my debts, taxes, funeral and testamentary expenses, and any other expenditures deemed necessary in connection with the administration of my estate. ---

4.   I give and bequeath the following specific legacies and donations:

(a) To each of my grandchildren living at the time of my death the sum of $5,000;

(b) To Woodside United Church, Dartmouth the sum of $500;

(c) To the Rotary Club of Dartmouth, the sum of $500;

(d) To my wife Mary Ann Fraser, my most recently acquired automobile;

(e) To my daughter Elizabeth Jane Wilson, the older of my automobiles;

(f) To my son Christopher Robert Fraser the cottage situated in the community of Chester Basin with the stipulation that my wife Mary Ann Fraser shall have full and complete unrestricted use thereof, during her lifetime. All cottage taxes, maintenance, repairs and expenditures thereon of every nature, including electricity, heat and care of the grounds, shall entirely be Christopher's responsibility.---

5.   I give and bequeath the residue of my estate to be divided among my wife and children and to my wife Mary Ann Fraser, if living at the time of my death and survives me by more than 15 days, fifty percent (one half). Should she predecease me or die within the aforesaid 15 days, the entire residue of my real and personal estate is to be divided by my executor into two equal parts and paid and delivered unto my two children, namely Elizabeth Jane and Christopher Robert. In the event my wife Mary Ann Fraser is living at the time of my death and survives me by more than 15 days, the remaining fifty percent of the residue of my Estate is to be divided by my executor into two equal parts and paid and delivered unto my two aforesaid children, namely Elizabeth Jane and Christopher Robert so that each receives twenty-five percent of the residue. --

6.   In the event any of my children predecease me, his quarter share shall be paid in equal parts to his children, who are living at the time of my death. The living children of the deceased parent shall receive equal portions of their parent's portion of the residue of my estate. In the event either of my children predecease me leaving no issue, then the portion for my surviving child is increased to include the deceased child's portion. ⸻

7.   If my wife is living at the time of my death my Registered Retirement Savings Plans are to be transferred to her as beneficiary in accordance with instructions I have given the carrier. ⸻

8.   I authorize my executor in her discretion to sell at such price and in such manner and from time to time any real and personal property forming part of my estate, except the cottage situated in, Chester Basin, and to execute and deliver to the purchasers thereof such deeds and other documents of transfer as may, in her opinion, be necessary for the purpose of completing such sale.⸻

9.   I direct that the payment of any monies which may be payable to any beneficiary hereunder during his or her minority may be made by my executor in such manner as she thinks best, either to one of the parents, or guardians of such beneficiaries and the receipt of any such parent or guardian shall be a discharge to my executor for all such payments.⸻

10.   I authorize my executor, in the division of my estate in the portions herein provided, to value in her uncontrolled discretion any assets forming part of my estate and I direct that any such valuation shall be binding upon all persons and corporations who may become interested in my estate. ⸻

11.   I direct that my executor in making investments shall not be restricted to investments in which trustees are authorized by law to invest funds, and I hereby relieve and exonerate my executor from all liability and for any loss that may be occasioned to my estate by reason of her so doing. ⸻

IN TESTIMONY WHEREOF I have to this my LAST WILL and Testament written upon this and one preceding page of paper, subscribed my name this 25th day of November A.D., 1993.

SIGNED by JAMES ROBERT FRASER,
the Testator, as and for his Last Will and
Testament, in the presence of us both
present at the same time, who, at his
request and in his presence, and in the
presence of each other have hereto
subscribed our names as witnesses.

Name: Glenn Holmes
Address : 969 Crichton Avenue,
            Dartmouth, Nova Scotia
Occupation : Sales Sifto Salt Co.

Name: Elizabeth Holmes
Address: 969 Crichton Avenue
            Dartmouth, Nova Scotia
Occupation: Nurse

JAMES ROBERT FRASER

PROVINCE OF NOVA SCOTIA)   IN THE COURT OF PROBATE

COUNTY OF HALIFAX   )   In the estate of JAMES ROBERT
                                             FRASER, deceased

I, MARY ANN FRASER, of Dartmouth, in the County of Halifax, Province of Nova Scotia make oath and say:

THAT I believe this paper writing hereto annexed, marked with the letter "A", to contain the true and original last will and testament, of James Robert Fraser, late of Dartmouth, in the County of Halifax, Province of Nova Scotia.

THAT I am the executor therein named, and that I will faithfully administer the property of the said testator by paying his just debts, legacies contained in his will, and the lawful expenses, so far as the same will thereunto extend and the law bind me, by distributing the residue (if any) of the estate according to law; and that I will make a full and true inventory of the real and personal property of the deceased, and exhibit the same unto the registry, upon oath, within three months from the date of the probate granted in this estate, or within such further time as is allowed by the court, and render a just and full account of executorship within eighteen months from the said date.

SWORN before me at Dartmouth,
in the County of Halifax,
and Province of Nova Scotia,
this 8th day of June
1996.

....
A Barrister of the Supreme
  Court of Nova Scotia

....
Mary Ann Fraser

PROVINCE OF NOVA SCOTIA)   **IN THE COURT OF PROBATE**
COUNTY OF HALIFAX   )

In the Estate of **JAMES ROBERT FRASER**, deceased.
The Petition of Mary Ann Fraser, of Dartmouth in the County of Halifax, Province of Nova Scotia, humbly showeth:

1.   **That** James Robert Fraser, died on or about the 24th day of May, 1996, at Dartmouth the County of Halifax, and that at the time of death the deceased had a fixed place of abode at Dartmouth, in the County of Halifax, Province of Nova Scotia.

2.   **THAT** the value of the whole property in respect to which this application is made which the deceased died possessed of or in any way entitled to is less that two hundred and seventy nine thousand dollars ($279,000); the value of the personal property and effects is less than two hundred and thirty-six thousand dollars ($236,000) and the value of the real property is less than forty-three thousand dollars ($43,000).

3.   **THAT** the real property is situate in the registration district of Chester, County of Lunenburg, Nova Scotia.

4.   **THAT** the deceased made a last will and testament bearing the date the 25th day of November, 1993.

5.   **THAT** your petitioner is the executrix named in the will.

Wherefore your petitioner humbly prays that the court may be pleased to grant probate of the will of the deceased to Mary Ann Fraser.

Dated the 8th day of June, 1996.

Mary A. Fraser
Mary Ann Fraser

EXHIBIT 4B: EXECUTOR'S AFFIDAVIT TO OPEN ESTATE (FORM E (SECTION 28), NOVA SCOTIA PROBATE ACT)

PROVINCE OF NOVA SCOTIA)   IN THE COURT OF PROBATE

COUNTY OF HALIFAX   )

In the estate of **JAMES ROBERT FRASER**, deceased.

     I, Mary ann Fraser, of Dartmouth, in the County of Halifax, make oath and say:

     1.   **THAT** I am the petitioner in the foregoing petition and have signed the same.

     2.   **THAT** the matters set out in paragraph 1 of the petition are true in substance and in fact and that all matters therein set out are true to the best of my knowledge, information and belief.

SWORN before me at Dartmouth,
in the County of Halifax,
Province of Nova Scotia,
this 8th day of June
1996

_____
A Barrister of the Supreme
   Court of Nova Scotia

_____
Mary Ann Fraser

AFFIDAVIT OF EXECUTION OF WILL

PROVINCE OF NOVA SCOTIA)   **IN THE COURT OF PROBATE**

COUNTY OF HALIFAX   **)**   In the estate of **JAMES ROBERT FRASER**, deceased.

I, Glenn Holmes, of Amherst in the County of Colchester, Province of Nova Scotia make oath and say:

1.   **THAT** I knew James Robert Fraser late of Dartmouth, in the County of Halifax, Province of Nova Scotia, deceased.

2.   **THAT** on or about the 25th day of November, 1993, I was personally present and did see the paper writing hereto annexed marked "A", signed by the said James Robert Fraser, as the same now appears as and for his last will and testament, and that the same was so signed by the said James Robert Fraser in the presence of me and of Elizabeth Holmes of the County of Colchester who were both present and at the same time; whereupon the said Elizabeth Holmes, and I did at the request of the said James Robert Fraser, and in his presence attest and subscribe the said will.

3.   **THAT** the said testator was then of sound and disposing mind, memory and understanding, and of the age of majority and upwards.

Sworn before me at......................,
in the County of..........................,
this .... day of........................
1996

....
Glenn Holmes

....

EXHIBIT 6: LETTER TO REGISTRAR WITH DOCUMENTS

*Note: The address for the Probate Court has changed to 1815 Upper Water St., Halifax, N.S., B3J 1S7. This address change also affects Exhibits 19, 27, and 35.

937 Crichton Avenue
Dartmouth, N. S.
B4A 4T7
Phone 469-5662

June 8, 1996

The Registrar
Probate Court, County of Halifax
1690 Hollis Street
Halifax, Nova Scotia
B3K 4G6

Dear Sir:

Estate of James Robert Fraser

I am the executor named in the last will of the late James Robert Fraser who died on May 24th, 1996, and his widow.

Enclosed are the following documents to open his estate:

> Petition for probate with will attached
> Oath of executrix
> Affidavit of witness to be signed by Glenn Holmes

Mr. Glenn Holmes and his wife Elizabeth are the witnesses who signed the will. Mr. Holmes has told me he will verify they witnessed James sign the will. The Holmes now live in Amherst, Nova Scotia at 235 Ocean View, Postal Code B6J 3B2. Their telephone number is 634-7843.

Mr. James Wilford, an accountant residing at 35 Delta Drive, Dartmouth, and Mr. Louis Belliveau, a bank manger residing at 64 Victoria Road, Dartmouth have agreed to appraise the value of the estate.

If you require any additional information, I shall be pleased to provide it. Please call me when I have been appointed executrix and let me know the amount of the probate fee. I will pay it when I come to receive the documents.

Please provide me with six certified copies of the Certificate of Probate and two Letters Testamentary.

Yours truly,

Mary A Fraser
Mary Ann Fraser

Canada   )
Province of Nova Scotia)   IN THE COURT OF PROBATE
County of Halifax   )

CERTIFICATE OF PROBATE

I, Susan E. Cole, of Halifax, in the County of Halifax, Registrar of Her Majesty's Court for the Probate of Wills and for Granting Letters of Administration within the said County of Halifax,

DO HEREBY CERTIFY to all whom it may Concern to Know:

That on the 20th day of June A.D.,1996, the LAST WILL AND TESTAMENT OF JAMES ROBERT FRASER, NO: 53694, late of Dartmouth, in the County of Halifax, who died at Dartmouth, in the County of Halifax, on the 24th day of May A.D. 1996, was Duly Proved before the said Court of Probate, and that thereupon Probate of the said Will was granted and Decreed by the said Court to Mary Ann Fraser, of Dartmouth in the County of Halifax, the Executor named in the Will, she being first duly sworn well and faithfully to execute said Will according to law and the true tenor thereof: also to file a full and true Inventory of the Goods and Estate of the said deceased, and to account for the same when thereto by law required.

I FURTHER CERTIFY that the said WILL is now in my custody as such Registrar, and that the same is duly recorded in the Registry of the said Court in Will Book 95, Page 307, and that Probate thereof, so granted as aforesaid, has not been revoked.

IN TESTIMONY WHEREOF, I have hereto subscribed my name and office, and have also affixed the Seal of the said Court at Halifax, aforesaid, this 20th day of June A.D. 1996.

Susan E. Cole

REGISTRAR OF PROBATE
SUSAN E. COLE

Susan E. Cole
Registrar of Probate
of the Probate District of
the County of Halifax

Canada   )
Province of Nova Scotia)   **IN THE COURT OF PROBATE**
County of Halifax   )

CERTIFICATE OF PROBATE

I, Susan E. Cole, of Halifax, in the County of Halifax, Registrar of Her Majesty's Court for the Probate of Wills and for Granting Letters of Administration within the said County of Halifax,

DO HEREBY CERTIFY to all whom it may Concern to Know:

That on the 20th day of June A.D.,1996, the **LAST WILL AND TESTAMENT OF JAMES ROBERT FRASER, NO: 53694,** late of Dartmouth, in the County of Halifax, who died at Dartmouth, in the County of Halifax, on the 24th day of May A.D. 1996, was Duly Proved before the said Court of Probate, and that thereupon Probate of the said Will was granted and Decreed by the said Court to Mary Ann Fraser, of Dartmouth in the County of Halifax, the Executor named in the Will, she being first duly sworn well and faithfully to execute said Will according to law and the true tenor thereof: also to file a full and true Inventory of the Goods and Estate of the said deceased, and to account for the same when thereto by law required.

I FURTHER CERTIFY that the said WILL is now in my custody as such Registrar, and that the same is duly recorded in the Registry of the said Court in Will Book 95, Page 307, and that Probate thereof, so granted as aforesaid, has not been revoked.

IN TESTIMONY WHEREOF, I have hereto subscribed my name and office, and have also affixed the Seal of the said Court at Halifax, aforesaid, this 20th day of June A.D. 1996.

(SGD) SUSAN E. COLE
REGISTRAR OF PROBATE

Province of Nova Scotia)   In the Court of Probate

County of Halifax   )   In the estate of JAMES ROBERT

                                               FRASER, deceased

Be it known that on the 20th day of June, 1996, the last will and testament of James Robert Fraser, in the County of Halifax, (a true copy of which is hereunder annexed), was proved, approved and registered in the registry of the court at Halifax, and said deceased having, whilst living,and at the time of his death, goods, chattels or credits within the said County, and a fixed place of abode therein, by reason whereof the proving and registering the said will, and granting administration of all and singular the said goods, chattels and credits, and also the auditing, allowing, and final discharging the accounts thereof, are well known to appertain to the court of probate in the said County: and that probate of the said will and administration of all and singular the goods, chattels, and credits of the said deceased, and any way concerning the said will, was granted to MARY ANN FRASER, having first duly sworn well and faithfully to administer the same by paying the just debts of the deceased, and the legacies contained in his will, and the lawful expenses, and by distributing the residue, if any, according to law, and to make a full and true inventory of all and singular the real property, goods, chattels, and credits of the deceased, and to exhibit and file the same in the registry of our court, upon oath, within three months from the date hereof, and also to render a just and true account thereof, and to do and perform all such other acts, matters and things, as to the true and faithful administration thereof may or shall lawfully appertain when thereunder required by law so to do.

Given at Halifax aforesaid, in the registry of the said court, under the seal thereof, the 20th day of June, 1996.

Susan E. Cole

REGISTRAR OF PROBATE

SUSAN E. COLE

WARRANT OF APPRAISEMENT

Province of Nova Scotia)   In the Court of Probate

County of Halifax   )   In the estate of JAMES
                                   ROBERT FRASER, deceased

To **Louis Belliveau**, bank manager, of Dartmouth, in the County of Halifax

and

To **Peter Wilford**, accountant, of Dartmouth, in the County of Halifax.

Greeting:

You are hereby appointed and empowered to take an inventory of all the real property, goods and effects of which James Robert Fraser late of Dartmouth in the County aforesaid, died seized or possessed within the Province, and truly and impartially, and according to the best of your knowledge and ability, to appraise the same, which, when completed, you are to deliver to the executor of the said deceased, to be returned, together with this warrant in three months from the date hereof.

Given under the seal of the court this 20th day of June, 1996.

Susan E. Cole

REGISTRAR OF PROBATE

SUSAN E. COLE

Province of Nova Scotia)   **In the Court of Probate**

County of Halifax   )   **In the estate of JAMES
                                   ROBERT FRASER, deceased**

We, Louis Belliveau and Peter Wilford of Dartmouth in the County of Halifax, the appraisers named in the warrant of appraisement in this estate, severally make oath and say:

That severally we will truly and impartially, and to the best of our knowledge and ability, appraise the real property, goods and effects exhibited to us, of which the said James Robert Fraser died seized or possessed within the Province.

The above-named Louis Belliveau)
and Peter Wilford were severally)
sworn before me this ....)
day of ...., 199......, at)
.............in the County of)
................,   )   ....
                                        Louis Belliveau

....

Peter Wilford

EXHIBIT 10B: APPRAISEMENT OF INVENTORY FORM (FORMS P (SECTION 38), NOVA SCOTIA PROBATE ACT)

INVENTORY

Province of Nova Scotia)
County of Halifax   )

In the Court of Probate
In the estate of JAMES
ROBERT FRASER, deceased

Inventory and valuation of the property of the said deceased.

General Description of Property

Value or Amount

General Description of Property	Value or Amount
Real property	
....	
Less encumbrances...	
Personal property	
....	
....	
....	
....	
....	
....	
....	
TOTAL $	

Dated this ...... day of ...., 19....

....
Louis Belliveau

....
Peter Wilford

....
Mary Ann Fraser

I, Mary Ann Fraser, make oath and say:

That I am the executrix.

That the above is to the best of my knowledge, information and belief, a true inventory and valuation of the property of the said deceased at the time of his death so far as I can at present ascertain.

Sworn before me at ....,
in the County of ....,
this ....day of ....,
19....

....
Mary Ann Fraser

....

EXHIBIT 11: LETTER TO ROYAL GAZETTE

937 Crichton Avenue
Dartmouth, N. S.
B3A 4T7

June 20, 1996

Office of the Royal Gazette
Department of Justice
5151 Terminal Road
Halifax, Nova Scotia
   B3J 2L6

ESTATE OF JAMES ROBERT FRASER

I am the executrix of the above estate and was granted Probate on June 20, 1996.
Please publish the required notice:

ESTATE OF: Fraser, James Robert
                        Dartmouth, Halifax County
                        June 20, 1996

Executor: Mary Ann Fraser
                        937 Crichton Avenue
                        Dartmouth, N. S.
                        B3A 4T7

Solicitor for the estate: None

A Certified Copy of Probate is presented with this letter. Please return it to me.

Yours truly

Mary A Fraser

Mary Fraser
Executor

EXHIBIT 12: ROYAL GAZETTE EXCERPT

<table>
<tr><td>Wednesday June 26, 1996</td><td>THE ROYAL GAZETTE</td><td>2956</td></tr>
</table>

ESTATE NOTICES

All persons having legal demands against any of the undernoted estates are requested to render the same, duly attested, within six months from the date of the first advertisement hereof: and all persons indebted to the said estate are required to make immediate payment to the executor noted.

ESTATE NOTICES BEING PUBLISHED FOR THE FIRST TIME

ESTATE OF: Date of Probate or Administration	Executor (Ex) or Administrator (Ad)	Solicitor or Proctor and Date of the First Insertion
CARPENTER, Stanley Louis Antigonish County July 7-95	Marie Vivian Carpenter (Ex) Havre Boucher Antigonish County, N.S. B0H 1P0	Duncan J. Chisholm Richard and MacDonald P.O. Box 1208 Antigonish, N.S. B2G 2L6 June 26-96 - (6m)
CORBETT, Annie Wolfville Ridge, Kings County June 27-96	Pauline Cavanagh (Ex) c/o Taylor, MacLellan & Cochrane P.O. Box 190 Kentville, N.S. B4N 3W4	James E. Dewar, Q.C. Taylor, MacLellan & Cochrane 50 Cornwallis Street P.O. Box 190 Kentville, N.S. B4N 3W4 June 26-96 - (6m)
DUFFNEY, William Pius South Bar Highway Cape Breton Regional Municipality July 11-96	Mary Josephine Duffney (Ex) c/o M. Joseph Rizzetto 269 Charlotte Street Sydney, N.S. B1P 1C4	M. Joseph Rizzetto 269 Charlotte Street Sydney, N.S. B1P 1C4 June 26-96 - (6m)
DUNN, Louise Alberta Brooklyn, Yarmouth County June 27-96	William Dunn (Ex) R.R.#1, Glenwood Yarmouth County, N.S. B0W 1W0	Patricia E. Caldwell, Q.C. Pink Macdonald Harding P.O. Drawer 398 379 Main Street Yarmouth, N.S. B5A 4B3 June 26-96 - (6m)
DUVERT, August Joseph Musquodoboit Harbour, Halifax County July 27-95	Danena Agnes Rowlings and Leonard W. Dunn (Exs) c/o Eastern Shore Law Centre P.O. Box 357 Musquodoboit Harbour, N.S. B0J 2L0	Myra L. Batalion Eastern Shore Law Centre P.O. Box 357 Musquodoboit Harbour, N.S. B0J 2L0 June 26-96 - (6m)
FRASER, James Robert Dartmouth, Halifax County June 20 - 96	Mary Ann Fraser (Ex.) 937 Crichton Avenue Dartmouth, N. S. B3A 4T7	June 26-96 - (6m)

937 Crichton Avenue
Dartmouth, N. S.
B3A 4T7

June 27, 1996

Mrs. Elizabeth Wilson
26 Humber Street
Halifax, N.S.
B6K 4M7

Dear Elizabeth:

In his will your father made $5,000 bequests to his grandchildren, living at the time of his death. While Joanne and Stanley are now under age, paragraph number 9 of the will states that the money can be paid to either of the parents, thereby eliminating the probable necessity of the estate holding the funds in trust for the children until they become of age. Enclosed are cheques payable to you, in trust:

> Number 8 $5,000 for Joanne Wilson
> Number 9 $5,000 for Stanley Wilson

The money should be invested in your name "IN TRUST" for each child until they reach their majority.

Please acknowledge receipt by signing and returning the copy of this letter.

Sincerely

Mary Fraser

Mary Fraser
Executor

I acknowledge receiving two cheques, each for $5,000 from The Estate of James Robert Fraser; in payment of legacies to my children Joanne Wilson and Stanley Wilson.

Date June 27, 1996   *Elizabeth Wilson*

Elizabeth Wilson

EXHIBIT 14, PAGE 1: DECLARATION OF TRANSMISSION

MONTREAL TRUST   STOCK AND BOND TRANSFER SERVICES

DECLARATION OF TRANSMISSION

ESTATE OF *JAMES ROBERT FRASER*

I/WE, THE UNDERSIGNED, *MARY ANN FRASER*

RESIDING AT *DARTMOUTH, NOVA SCOTIA* AND ACTING IN MY/OUR

QUALITY AS *EXECUTOR* AND HAVING KNOWLEDGE OF THE FACTS PERTAINING TO THE ESTATE AND DO HEREBY SOLEMNLY DECLARE:

1. THAT THE LATE *JAMES ROBERT FRASER*

   IN HIS/HER LIFETIME OF *DARTMOUTH*

   DIED ON THE *24th* DAY OF *MAY* 19 *96*.

2. THE SAID DECEASED WAS NEVER/ONLY *ONCE* MARRIED, NAMELY, TO THE FOLLOWING PERSON(S) *MARY ANN FRASER* ;

   (1) FROM WHOM S(HE) WAS SEPARATE AS TO PROPERTY BY REASON OF:

   A) MARRIAGE CONTRACT DATED _____

   BEFORE _____, NOTARY PUBLIC;

   B) THE LAWS OF THE *PROVINCE* OF *NOVA SCOTIA* WHERE

   THE SAID *MARY ANN FRASER* WAS DOMICILED AT THE TIME
   (NAME OF SPOUSE)   OF THE MARRIAGE, OR

   (II) WITH WHOM S(HE) WAS COMMON AS TO PROPERTY IN ACCORDANCE WITH THE LAWS

   OF THE _____ OF _____ WHERE

   THE SAID _____ WAS DOMICILED AT THE TIME OF THE
   (NAME OF SPOUSE)
   MARRIAGE, THERE BEING NO ANTE-NUPTIAL MARRIAGE CONTRACT STIPULATING SEPARATION AS TO PROPERTY;

   (III) WITH WHOM S(HE) WAS MARRIED UNDER PARTNERSHIP OF ACQUESTS IN ACCORDANCE WITH

   QUEBEC ONLY   THE LAWS OF THE _____ OF _____ WHERE

   THE SAID _____ WAS DOMICILED AT THE TIME OF THE
   (NAME OF SPOUSE)
   MARRIAGE, THERE BEING NO ANTE-NUPTIAL MARRIAGE CONTRACT STIPULATING SEPARATION AS TO PROPERTY AND THE SPOUSES HAVING BEEN MARRIED AFTER JULY 1, 1970.

   (IV) THE DECEASED WAS A WIDOWER/WIDOW AT THE TIME OF DEATH, HIS/HER LAST CONSORT DIED PRIOR TO THE ISSUANCE OF THE CERTIFICATE(S) HEREWITH TRANSFERRED,

   NAMELY, ON _____

3. THE DECEASED, HAVING LEFT AS HIS/HER

   A) ONLY TESTAMENTARY DISPOSITION A WILL AND CODICIL(S) ADMITTED TO PROBATE

   IN THE *PROBATE* COURT, DISTRICT OF *HALIFAX N.S.*

   ON THE *20th* DAY OF *JUNE* 19 *96*.

   COPY OF SAID WILL AND CODICIL(S) AND PROBATE, CERTIFIED UNDER SEAL OF SAID COURT, BEING ATTACHED HERETO;

   B) ONLY TESTAMENTARY DISPOSITION A WILL EXECUTED BEFORE _____

   _____, NOTARY, ON THE _____ DAY OF _____ 19 _____ AND A CODICIL

   THERETO EXECUTED BEFORE _____, NOTARY, ON THE _____

   DAY OF _____ 19 _____

4. THAT THE DECEASED DIED AB INTESTATE:

   A) LEAVING AS HIS/HER SOLE HEIRS THE UNDER-MENTIONED PERSONS, NAMELY:

   _____

   _____

   _____

   (PLEASE STATE RELATIONSHIP)

P 3142 E

EXHIBIT 14, PAGE 2: DECLARATION OF TRANSMISSION

B) LETTERS OF ADMINISTRATION OF HIS/HER ESTATE WERE GRANTED BY

*FOR USE IN ESTATES
OUTSIDE OF QUEBEC* _____

(DESCRIPTION OF COURT)

TO _____

ON THE _____ DAY OF _____ 19 _____ ;

5. THAT THE FOLLOWING ARE APPOINTED EXECUTORS OF THE DECEASED:

____MARY ANN FRASER_____

_____

6. THAT THE DECEASED WAS AT THE TIME OF HIS/HER DEATH THE BENEFICIAL OWNER ON THE BOOKS

OF _____

OF ITS _____, REPRESENTED BY CERTIFICATE(S)

(DESCRIPTION OF SECURITY)

NUMBERED _____ ;

7. THAT THE LATE _____ AND THE PERSON OR PERSONS
NAMED IN THE CERTIFICATE IS/ARE ONE AND THE SAME;

8. FOR PURPOSES OF THE SUCCESSION DUTY ACT IN QUEBEC, PLEASE INDICATE ONE OF THE FOLLOWING:

☐ DISPOSAL PERMIT ENCLOSED.

☐ THE _____HEREWITH TRANSMITTED
DID NOT EXCEED A MARKET VALUE OF $1,500.00 AT THE DATE OF DEATH,
THEREFORE UNDER SECTION 55R1(2) OR (3) OF THE REGULATIONS RESPECT-
ING THE APPLICATION OF THE SUCCESSION DUTY ACT, NO DISPOSAL
PERMIT IS REQUIRED.

☐ THE DECEASED AND THE BENEFICIARY(IES) WERE RESIDENT AND DOMI-
CILED OUTSIDE THE PROVINCE OF QUEBEC AT THE TIME OF DEATH OF THE
SHAREHOLDER, THEREFORE, UNDER SECTION 55R1(4) OF THE REGULA-
TIONS RESPECTING THE APPLICATION OF THE SECCESSION DUTY ACT, NO
DISPOSAL PERMIT IS REQUIRED.

9. BY VIRTUE OF THE FOREGOING, THE SAID SECURITIES HAVE DEVOLVED UPON AND BECOME VESTED IN
THIS/THESE DECLARANT(S) AS EXECUTOR(S), LEGATEES(S), HEIR(S)-AT-LAW, AS AFORESAID, AND THIS/
THESE DECLARANT(S) DESIRE(S) TO HAVE THE SAME

RECORDED IN THE NAME OF _____

_____

_____

(COMPLETE ADDRESS)

AND I/WE MAKE THIS SOLEMN DECLARATION, CONSCIENTIOUSLY BELIEVING IT TO BE TRUE AND
KNOWING THAT IT IS OF THE SAME FORCE AND EFFECT AS IF MADE UNDER OATH AND BY VIRTUE OF **THE
CANADA EVIDENCE ACT.**

DECLARED BEFORE ME

AT _HALIFAX_____

THIS _14_ DAY OF _July_ 19 _96_____

DECLARANT

Mary A. Fraser

_____   _____

A COMMISSIONER OF OATHS
NOTARY PUBLIC   _____

(PLEASE AFFIX SEAL OF OFFICE)   _____

**POWER OF ATTORNEY
TO TRANSFER SECURITIES**

FOR VALUE RECEIVED the undersigned hereby sells, assigns and transfers to

_____
(Name of Transferee)

of _____
(Address)

the following securities:

(a) _____*1,000 shares*_____ shares of _*The Bank of Nova*_
(Number of shares)   (Class/Shares & Name of Issuer)

_*Scotia, Common*_____

OR

$_____   _____%

_____

(Description of bonds, debentures, notes, certificates of deposit
or other securities and name of Issuer)

standing in the name of the undersigned and hereby irrevocably appoints

_____
(This space should be left blank)

the attorney of the undersigned to transfer the said securities on the books of the said Issuer with full power of substitution.

*July 14 1996*
(Date)

ESTATE OF JAMES R. FRASER

Witnessed by

*George Anderson*   Per _*Mary A. Fraser*_
(Signature of Witness)   **Executor**

(Signature of Transferor)

Signature of Transferor is
hereby guaranteed by

ESTATE OF JAMES R. FRASER

RECEIPTS - MONEY RECEIVED

DATE	PARTICULARS	AMOUNT	TOTALS
1996			
June 21	Sale coin collection - Johnson's Coins	2,500.00	2,500.00
	Jim's final pay cheque	1,765.13	4,265.13
	Jim's CSB instalment purchase refund	875.00	5,140.13
	Income tax refund for 1995	305.00	5,445.13
27	Transfer Bank Montreal checking a/c #3461-7	3,541.67	8,986.80
	Bank Montreal GIC due July 4,1996	15,000.00	23,986.80
	Interest on GIC @ 6.5% from July 4/95	892.14	24,878.94
30	Bank interest on estate account	1.15	24,880.09
July 6	Life insurance Commercial Travellers	3,125.00	28,005.09
	Canada Pension Plan death benefit	3,540.00	31,545.09
8	Car insurance refunds	438.90	31,983.99
15	Car licences refunds from Province	96.00	32,079.99
26	Dividend - 1,000 shs Bank of Nova Scotia	340.00	32,419.99
31	Bank interest	22.82	32,442.81
Aug. 5	From Acadia Investments May 24 balance $4,214.18		
	plus $13.98 interest and $945 dividends		
	earned since then	5,173.16	37,615.97
15	Dividend - 1,000 shs Nova Scotia Power	200.00	37,815.97
31	Bank interest	34.89	37,850.86
Sep. 30	Bank interest	35.07	37,885.93
Oct. 15	Proceeds from sale securities by Acadian	205,745.00	243,630.93
26	Dividend - 1,000 shs Bank of Nova Scotia	340.00	243,970.93
31	Bank interest	37.90	244,008.83
Nov. 1	Interest Canada Savings Bonds	1,350.00	245,358.83
	Canada Savings Bonds cashed	25,000.00	270,358.83
30	Bank interest	54.10	270,412.93
Dec. 31	Bank interest	54.21	270,467.14
1997			
Jan. 31	Bank interest	54.97	270,522.11
Feb. 28	Bank interest	55.20	270,577.31
Mar. 31	Bank interest	51.08	270,628.39
Apr. 30	Bank interest	41.67	270,670.06
May 31	Bank interest	41.71	270,711.77
Jun. 30	Bank interest	41.74	270,753.51
Jul. 31	Bank interest	41.77	270,795.28

EXHIBIT 16B: ACCOUNTING FOR PAYMENTS

ESTATE OF JAMES R. FRASER

DISBURSEMENTS - EXPENSES

DATE		CK.NO.	PARTICULARS	AMOUNT	TOTALS
1996					
June	21	1	Mary Fraser recovery of Probate fee	1,050.00	1,050.00
		2	Mary Fraser recovery-ad in Royal Gazette	32.10	1,082.10
	27	3	City Funeral Home Ltd.	5,566.50	6,648.60
		4	Sackville Cemetery fo plot	1,500.00	8,148.60
		5	County of Lunenburg cottage tax	246.00	8,394.60
		6	Rotary Club of Dartmouth	500.00	8,894.60
		7	Woodside United Church	500.00	9,394.60
		8	Elizabeth Wilson in trust for daughter Joanne Wilson	5,000.00	14,394.60
		9	Elizabeth Wilson in trust for son Stanley Wilson	5,000.00	19,394.60
	23	10	Richard E. Clarke, Q.C. for Probate documents	214.00	19,608.60
		11	Bank of Montreal Mastercard Jim's account	697.60	20,306.20
July	12	12	Vacation Real Estate Ltd. cottage appraisal	100.00	20,406.20
	13	13	Registry of Motor Vehicles - licences	222.00	20,628.20
	29	14	Richard E. Clarke,Q.C. for transfer of Chester Basin		20,628.20
			cottage to Christopher	342.67	20,970.87
Aug.	15	15	Registrar of Probate additional fee	105.00	21,075.87
		16	Louis Belliveau for appraisal	75.00	21,150.87
		17	Peter Wilford for appraisal	75.00	21,225.87
Sep.	20	18	Richard E. Clarke,Q.C. affidavits for appraisement		21,225.87
			of inventory	65.00	21,290.87
Oct.	7	19	Hilltop Monuments Limited	2,139.00	23,429.87
	15	20	Revenue Canada - Jim's final income tax return for		23,429.87
			May 24, 1996	26,259.11	49,688.98
	20	21	Elizabeth Wilson partial distribution	45,000.00	94,688.98
		22	Christopher Fraser partial distribution	45,000.00	139,688.98
		23	Mary Fraser partial distribution	90,000.00	229,688.98
	28	24	Peter Wilford preparing May 24, 1996 tax return	200.00	229,888.98
1997					229,888.98
Mar.	24	25	Revenue Canada tax Estate return December 31, 1996	7,257.33	237,146.31
May 28		26	Minister of Finance for Royal Gazette ad	16.05	237,162.36
June	20	27	Richard E. Clarke, Q.C. for documents	271.50	237,433.86
		28	Peter Wilford for accounting report to close estate	215.00	237,648.86
July	15	29	Registrar of Probate estate closing fee	632.00	238,280.86
	18	30	Mary Fraser postage June 2 registered letters	7.15	238,288.01
Aug.	12	31	Peter Wilford for final estate tax return	157.50	238,445.51
		32	Elizabeth Wilson 25% of residue	8,087.44	246,532.95
		33	Christopher Fraser 25% of residue	8,087.44	254,620.39
		34	Mary Fraser 50% of residue	16,174.89	270,795.28

CHESTER BASIN COTTAGE AGREEMENT

Mary Ann Fraser, executor of the Estate of James Robert Fraser, deceased, and Christopher Robert Fraser, son of the deceased, hereinafter referred to as the "parties", have entered into this agreement to formally record their responsibilities with regards to the bequest made to Christopher Robert Fraser in the last will of the Late James Robert Fraser. Under the terms of the will ownership of the family cottage and grounds on which it is located in Chester Basin, County of Lunenburg herein after called the "property", is given to Christopher Robert Fraser, with Mary Ann Fraser retaining full occupancy rights. In this connection the two parties have agreed to the following terms and conditions:

1. Mary Ann Fraser shall have full and complete unrestricted use of the Property during her lifetime;

2. All structural repairs, maintenance, grounds maintenance and expenditures to adequately maintain the property, including electricity, heating and care of the grounds shall completely be for the account of, and at the expense of Christopher Robert Fraser;

3. In the event of any unresolved dispute between the parties to this agreement either of them shall have the right to have the dispute submitted for arbitration. Each of them shall appoint one person to be their representative and the two representatives shall chose a third person, and the three of them shall be the Arbitration Committee. The decision of the Arbitration Committee shall be final and binding on both parties with each of them paying one half the cost of the arbitration.

4. Christopher Robert Fraser undertakes not to sell or mortgage the property or permit any encumbrances to be placed on it without the prior written consent of Mary Ann Fraser.

5. Christopher Robert Fraser hereby grants to Mary Ann Fraser an option to purchase the property, to be exercised only in the event of his demise thirty days or more prior to her demise. In that event Mary Ann Fraser shall have the right to purchase the property and all contents from his estate for the lessor of it's readily net sale value, or the amount of one hundred and forty five thousand dollars ($145,000.00).

Dated this 25th day of July, 1996:

_____
Witness

_____
Witness

_____
Christopher Robert Fraser

_____
Mary Ann Fraser

EXHIBIT 18: APPRAISEMENT OF INVENTORY, COMPLETE (FORMS P (SECTION 38), NOVA SCOTIA PROBATE ACT)

INVENTORY

Province of Nova Scotia)   In the Court of Probate
County of Halifax   )   In the estate of JAMES
                                                        ROBERT FRASER, deceased

Inventory and valuation of the property of the said deceased.

General Description of Property

	Value or Amount
Real property _Cottage in Chester Basin,_	
Lunenburg, N.S.	144,760
Less encumbrances	—
Personal property	
Bank accounts	26,257
Investments	197,569
Vehicles	22,160
Accounts receivable	7,020
Life Insurance	3,125
(See attached schedule "A" for details)	
TOTAL	$ 256,131

Dated this 14th day of August, 1996

L. Belliveau
Louis Belliveau

Mary A. Fraser
Mary Ann Fraser

C. Wilford
Peter Wilford

I, Mary Ann Fraser, make oath and say:

That I am the executrix.

That the above is to the best of my knowledge, information and belief, a true inventory and valuation of the property of the said deceased at the time of his death so far as I can at present ascertain.

Sworn before me at _Dartmouth_
in the County of _Halifax_
this 14th day of _August_,
1996

R.J. Blanchard

Mary A. Fraser
Mary Ann Fraser

**A Barrister of the Supreme
Court of Nova Scotia**

EXHIBIT 18, SCHEDULE A: VALUATION OF INVENTORY, DETAILED LISTING

August 10, 1996

ESTATE OF ROBERT JAMES FRASER

INVENTORY AND VALUATION

MAY 24, 1996

REAL PROPERTY		APPRAISED VALUE
Cottage in Chester Basin, Nova Scotia		$144,760.00
(no encumbrances)		
TOTAL VALUATION OF REAL PROPERTY		**$144,760.00**

PERSONAL PROPERTY

BANK AND CREDIT ACCOUNTS		
Bank of Montreal, George St, Halifax:		
Chequing #3461-7	3,675.25	
Coin collection	2,500.00	
GIC 6.5%, due July 4, 1996	15,000.00	
Accrued interest to May 24	867.75	
Acadia Investments Inc.	4,214.18	26,257.18
INVESTMENTS		
500 shs Air Canada, com.	2,125.00	
2,000 shs Canadian Pacific, com.	48,500.00	
2,000 shs Maritime Tel & Tel, com.	42,000.00	
500 shs Nortel, com.	32,750.00	
1,000 shs Bank of Nova Scotia, com.	32,500.00	
10,000 shs Menora Resources Inc.	2,600.00	
1,000 shs Nova Scotia Power, com.	11,250.00	
$25,000 Canada Savings Bonds Series R46	25,000.00	
Accrued interest to May 24	843.75	197,568.75
VEHICLES		
1995 Buick Century four door	17,600.00	
1991 Honda Civic four door	4,560.00	22,160.00
ACCOUNT RECEIVABLE		
Telephone Company, final pay cheque	1,765.13	
Income tax refund for 1995	305.00	
Refund of CSB payroll payments	875.00	
Car insurance refunds	438.90	
Car licences refund	96.00	
Canada Pension death benefit	3,540.00	7,020.03
LIFE INSURANCE		
Commercial Travellers Association	3,125.00	3,125.00

TOTAL VALUATION OF PERSONAL PROPERTY		**$256,130.96**

937 Crichton Avenue
Dartmouth, N. S.
B3A 4T7

Phone 469-5662

August 14, 1996

Mrs. Susan E. Cole, Registrar
Probate Court of the District of Halifax County
1690 Hollis Street
Halifax, N. S.
B3K 4G6

Dear Mrs. Cole:

Estate of James Robert Fraser No. 53694

Enclosed are the completed **WARRANT OF APPRAISEMENT and APPRAISEMENT OF INVENTORY** documents for the estate. Personal property has been appraised at $ 256,130.96 and real property at $144,760. An opening fee of $980.00 was paid on June 20th based on a personal property estimated valuation of $236,000.

Is there an additional fee? If so, please tell me what it is,

Yours truly,

Mary A Fraser

Mary A. Fraser

EXHIBIT 20, PAGE 1: INCOME TAX RETURN—JAMES FRASER

```
File : FRASER      Name : James Robert Fraser        SIN : 414 712 216
 ---   Revenue
 : :   Canada                                         T1 GENERAL 1995
 ---
FEDERAL AND NOVA SCOTIA            FINAL RETURN                 ---
INDIVIDUAL INCOME TAX RETURN                                   : 7 :
STEP 1 - IDENTIFICATION                                        ---
Title:    Mr.                     Your SIN              414 712 216
First name: James Robert                                DD MM YY
Last name:  Fraser                Your date of birth:   21/02/34
Addr.: 37 Crichton Avenue         Your language of correspondence:
City:  Dartmouth                      English  (X) Français   (_)
Prov.: Nova Scotia                If this return is for
Postal code: B3A 4T7              a deceased person,    DD MM YY
                                  enter the date of death: 24/05/96
                                  On December 31, 1995, you were:
                                  1 (X) Married      2 (_) Common-law
                                  3 (_) Widowed      4 (_) Divorced
Province of residence Dec. 31, 1995:  5 (_) Separated    6 (_) Single
 NOVA SCOTIA                      Spouse's SIN:          113 981 468
                                  First name of your spouse:
Province of self-employment in 1995:  Mary A.
                                  Check this box if your spouse was
 —                                self-employed in 1995:     1 (_)
                                  ----------------------------------
Resident of Canada - part of 1995   : : : : :
         DD MM              DD MM  ----------------------------------
Date   entry: _____  departure: _____
STEP 2 - GOODS AND SERVICES TAX (GST) CREDIT
Are you applying for the goods and services tax credit ? Yes( _ )1   No( X )2
If yes, number of children under age 19 on December 31, 1995    —
If yes, your spouse's net income                            _____
STEP 3 - TOTAL INCOME
Employment income                           101    28,765.13
Commissions                          102  _____
Other employment income                     104  _____
Old Age Security pension                    113  _____
Canada or Québec Pension Plan benefits      114    3,540.00
Disability benefits              152  _____
Other pensions or superannuation            115  _____
Unemployment Insurance benefits             119  _____
Taxable amount of dividends                 120    3,556.25
Interest and other investment income        121    1,732.80
Net partnership income                      122  _____
Rental income        Gross 160 _____  Net 126  _____
Taxable capital gains                       127   50,388.75
Alimony or maintenance income               128  _____
RRSP income                                 129  _____
Other income: _____        130  _____
Business income   Gross 162 _____ Net 135  _____
Profession        Gross 164 _____ Net 137  _____
Commission        Gross 166 _____ Net 139  _____
Farming income    Gross 168 _____ Net 141  _____
Fishing income    Gross 170 _____ Net 143  _____
Workers' Compensation pmts    144 _____
Social assistance payments    145 _____
Net federal supplements       146 _____
   Add lines 144, 145 and 146. _____ > 147  _____
                       TOTAL INCOME 150    87,982.93

 605 :____:____:____:____:    600 :____:____:____:____:
     :____:____:____:____:        :____:____:____:____:
```

EXHIBIT 20, PAGE 2: INCOME TAX RETURN—JAMES FRASER

```
File : FRASER        Name : James Robert Fraser         SIN : 414 712 216
STEP 6 - REFUND OR BALANCE OWING                                          4
                                                 FEDERAL TAX 406     18,680.72
Political contributions          409 _____
Political contributions tax credit          410 _____ ¢
Investment tax credit (T2038)               412 _____ ¢
Labour-sponsored funds Net cost 413 _____
                    Allowable credit 414 _____ ¢
         Add lines 410, 412 and 414. 416          NIL >              NIL
Federal tax before federal individual surtax     417         18,680.72
Federal individual surtax                        419            869.46
           Add lines 417 and 419.  NET FEDERAL TAX 420       19,550.18
Canada Pension Plan contributions (self-employed) 421   _____
Social benefits repayment                        422    _____
Provincial tax          NOVA SCOTIA              428         11,226.53
           Add lines 420 through 428.  TOTAL PAYABLE 435     30,776.71¢


Total income tax deducted                437       4,517.60 ¢


Canada Pension Plan overpayment              448 _____ ¢
Unemployment Insurance overpayment           450 _____ ¢
Refund of investment tax credit (T2038)      454 _____ ¢
Part XII.2 trust tax credit (T3)             456 _____ ¢
Employee and partner GST rebate (GST-370)    457 _____ ¢
Tax paid by instalments                      476 _____ ¢
Forward-averaging tax credit (T581)          478 _____ ¢
Credits N.S.                                 479 _____ ¢


                 TOTAL CREDITS 482     4,517.60 >      4,517.60
            Subtract line 482 from line 435.          26,259.11
                                                 ============
      REFUND 484 _____ ¢    BALANCE OWING 485  26,259.11 ¢
                                   AMOUNT ENCLOSED 486   26,259.11 ¢
DIRECT DEPOSIT REQUEST
Branch      Institution                 Attach a cheque or money order
number      number    Account number    payable to the Receiver
702 _____   703 ___   704 _____   General. Your payment is due no
701 ( _ ) Child Tax Benefit (CTB)        later than April 30, 1997.
```

I certify that the information given on this return and in any documents
attached is correct, complete and fully discloses all my income.

Sign here *Mary A. Fraser* Date 15/10/96 Telephone (902) 469-5662

490 Person or firm paid to prepare this return.
Name _____ _____
Addr. _____ _____
Prov. _____ Postal code_____ Tel. _____

```
Do not use   639  |__|   |__|___|_|  |__|___|_|  |__|___|_|  |__|_|_|_|_| ¢
this area    684  |__|   |__|___|_|  |__|___|_|  |__|___|_|  |__|_|_|_|_|
```

RC-95-103

937 Crichton Avenue
Dartmouth, N. S.
B3A 4T7

October 20, 1996

Mrs. Elizabeth Jane Wilson
26 Humber Street
Halifax, N. S.
    B6K 4M7

Dear Elizabeth:

You are one of the residual beneficiaries of your father's will. Under the terms of the will you are to receive 25% of residue of the estate. At present the final residue amount is not known, but as executrix I am prepared to make partial distributions now.

Enclosed is cheque number 20 payable to you for $45,000.00.

Please acknowledge receipt by signing the duplicate of this letter.

Sincerely,

Mary A. Fraser.

Estate of James Robert Fraser
Mary A. Fraser, Executrix

I acknowledge receiving a cheque for $45,000 from the estate of James Robert Fraser.

Date October 20, 1996   *Elizabeth Wilson*

Elizabeth Jane Wilson

937 Crichton Avenue
Dartmouth, N. S.
B3A 4T7

October 20, 1996

Mr. Christopher Robert Fraser
1647 Sumer Street
Halifax, N. S.
   B7K 2H7

Dear Christopher:

You are one of the residual beneficiaries of your father's will. Under the terms of
the will you are to receive 25% of residue of the estate. At present the final
residue amount is not known, but as executrix I am prepared to make a partial
distributions now.

Enclosed is cheque number 21 payable to you for $45,000.00.

Please acknowledge receipt by signing the duplicate of this letter.

Sincerely,

Mary A. Fraser.

Estate of James Robert Fraser
Mary A. Fraser, Executrix

I acknowledge receiving a cheque for $45,000 from the estate of James Robert
Fraser.

Date October 20, 1996   *C R Fraser*
                      Christopher Robert Fraser

937 Crichton Avenue
Dartmouth, N. S.
B3A 4T7

October 20, 1996

Mrs. Mary Ann Fraser
37 Crichton Avenue
Dartmouth, N.S.
B3A 4T7

You are one of the residual beneficiaries of James Robert Fraser's will. Under the terms of the will you are to receive 50% of residue of the estate. At this point in time the residue amount is not known, but as executrix I am making a partial distribution.

Enclosed is cheque number 22 payable to you for $90,000.00.

Sincerely,

Mary A Fraser

Estate of James Robert Fraser
Mary A. Fraser, executrix

I acknowledge receiving a cheque for $90,000 from the estate of James Robert Fraser.

Date October 20, 1996   *Mary A Fraser*
                              MARY ANN FRASER

EXHIBIT 22: TAX CLEARANCE CERTIFICATE REQUESTED

Revenue Canada   Revenu Canada

TX19
Rev. 95

REQUEST FOR CLEARANCE CERTIFICATE

FOR DEPARTMENTAL USE ONLY

- This form is to be used where the "responsible representative" for an estate, business or property is requesting a clearance certificate as required by subsection 159(2) of the Income Tax Act. Responsible representative means the executor, administrator, trustee or similar person other than a trustee in bankruptcy.

- For more information, see the current version of IC 82-6, Requesting Clearance Certificates for Estates and Trusts, IT-282, Estate or Trust Distributions – Clearance Certificates or IT-368, Corporate Distributions - Clearance Certificates.

- This form should not be sent to the Department until:
  1. All required returns are filed and assessed.
  2. All taxes, contributions, interest and penalties have been paid or secured.

- This form is to be sent to the Business Audit Section at the district taxation office of the responsible representative, not the taxation centre.

IDENTIFICATION AREA

Name of Taxpayer
JAMES   ROBERT   FRASER

Address
937 CRICHTON   AVENUE, DARTMOUTH,   N.S.

Social Insurance Number, Corporation Account Number or Trust Number as applicable	Date of Birth	Date of Death
414 712 216	*FEB. 21, 1934*	*MAY 24, 1996*

Name of Responsible Representative
MARY   A. FRASER

Attention

Address
937 CRICHTON   AVENUE, DARTMOUTH,   N.S.   B3A 4T7

Capacity of Above	Telephone Number
EXECUTRIX	*(902) 469-5662*

Note: If there is more than one responsible representative, attach a separate list.

RETURNS FILED

Type of Return (✓ applicable box(es) if filed)		Period Covered	Date of Notice of Assessment
T1 "ordinary return"	✓	*Jan. 1, 1996 – May 24/96*	*Mar. 31, 1997*
T1 "rights and things"	☐		
T1 "trust income"	☐		
T1 "business income"	☐		
T2 Corporation Return	☐		
T3 Trust Return	☐		
Other (specify):			

ADDITIONAL INFORMATION REQUIRED

1. Date chosen for winding up the trust or corporation and distribution of assets . . . . _____

2. Clearance certificate requested (✓ one): TX21 FINAL ☐   TX21A DEATH ☐   TX21B PARTIAL ☑

Attach, if applicable and not previously provided:

3. ☑ Copy of the will (codicil, renunciations, and/or disclaimers) and all probate documents. Where the taxpayer died intestate, attach details of the proposed distribution of assets, name, address and S.I.N. of each beneficiary and relationship to the deceased.

4. ☐ Copy of Trust Document.

5. ☑ Statement showing the assets and distribution plan. For each asset, provide description, adjusted cost base and fair market value at date of death or distribution (in case of a partial distribution, the assets intended for distribution should be identified).

6. ☐ Letter of authorization allowing Revenue Canada, Taxation to communicate with the responsible representative about the taxpayer's affairs

---

CERTIFICATION AND UNDERTAKING

In my capacity as the *executor* _____ (eg. executor, administrator, trustee) of the taxpayer named in the IDENTIFICATION AREA, I am requesting a clearance certificate from the Minister certifying that all amounts for which that taxpayer is liable under the Income Tax Act in respect of the taxation year in which the distribution is made, or any preceding year, have been paid or that security for the payment has been accepted by the Minister. I undertake to complete the actual distribution of all of the property as soon as possible after the clearance certificate is received.

Date ___*April 8, 1997*___   Signature *Mary A Fraser*

Form prescribed by order of the Minister of National Revenue

(Français au verso)

EXHIBIT 23: INCOME TAX RETURN—LETTER

937 Crichton Avenue
Dartmouth, N. S.
B3A 4T7

April 8, 1997

Phone 902-469-5662

Business Audit Section
Revenue Canada Taxation Centre
Freshwater and Empire Ave.,
St. John's, NFLD.
A1B 3Z3

**The late James Robert Fraser
Number 414 712 216**

Enclosed is a REQUEST FOR CLEARANCE CERTIFICATE. Notices of assessment have been received up to and including date of death and all taxes have been paid.

A copy of Letters Testamentary with copy of will attached is enclosed, and also a copy of the inventory which was provided to the Court of Probate on August 14, 1996.

With the exception of the Chester Basin property and the two cars, the estate's assets have been converted to cash and will be distributed according to the will. The Chester Basin property had a fair market value on May 24, 1996 of $144,760 and ownership has been transferred to the deceased's son, Christopher Fraser. Ownership of the cars has been transferred as instructed in the will. The residue of the estate will be distributed as required by the will, to our two children and me.

Yours truly

Mary A Fraser

Mary Fraser
Executrix

EXHIBIT 24, PAGE 1: INCOME TAX RETURN—ESTATE'S RETURN

Revenue   Revenu
Canada   Canada

T3 1995

For departmental use

EXHIBIT 24, PAGE 1

TRUST INCOME TAX AND INFORMATION RETURN

Step I - Identification

Name of trust	Account number
ESTATE OF JAMES ROBERT FRASER	T

Name of trustee, executor, or administrator
MARY FRASER

Mailing address of trustee, executor, or administrator	Telephone number
937 CRICHTON AVENUE	(902) 469-5662
	Postal code
DARTMOUTH , N.S.	B3A 4T7

Residence of trust at end of taxation year
Province or territory   NOVA SCOTIA

If the trust had business income in the year, state province(s) or territory(ies) where that income was earned.

Was the trust resident in Canada throughout the taxation year?

Yes ☒   No ☐   If no, country _____

Type of trust

Testamentary

Date of death
19 96 05 24
Year Month Day

1. ☒ Spousal
Social insurance number of deceased
4 1 4 7 1 2 2 1 6

2. ☐ Other

Inter vivos

1. ☐ Spousal   8. ☐ Non-profit organization
2. ☐ Unit   Corporation account number, if it applies
3. ☐ Mutual fund
4. ☐ Communal organization   9. ☐ Employee trust
5. ☐ Employee benefit plan   10. ☐ Other inter vivos (specify)

Insurance segregated fund

6. ☐ Fully/Partially registered
Date trust created
7. ☐ Non-registered   19 ___ ___ ___
                         Year Month Day

Return for taxation year

from 19 96 05 24 to 19 96 12 31
       Year Month Day   Year Month Day

Is this the first year of filing a T3 return?   No ☐   Yes ☒

If no, for what year was the last return filed?
If yes, attach a copy of the trust document or will, and a list of assets at death (unless filed with the deceased's T1 return).   Attached ☒   With T1 ☐   Year

Is this an amended return?   No ☒   Yes ☐

Address on last return is same as above   Yes
or

Is this the final return of the trust?   No ☒   Yes ☐

If yes, give the date the trust wound up, or is planning to wind up.   19 ___ ___ ___
                                                                          Year Month Day

	No	Yes
1. Is the trust one of a number of trusts created from contributions by the same individual? If yes, attach a list of names, addresses, and account numbers of the other trusts.	☒	☐
2. For any trust (other than a unit trust) did the ownership of capital or income interests change since 1984? If yes, state the year, and if during this taxation year, attach a statement showing the changes.	☒	☐
3. Were the terms of the trust amended or varied since June 18, 1971? If yes, state the year, and if during this taxation year, attach copies of the documents effecting these changes.	☒	☐
4. Has the trust continuously resided in Canada since it was established (or since June 18, 1971, if it was established before that date)?	☐	☒
5. Did the trust receive any capital additions by way of a gift since June 18, 1971? If yes, state the year, and if during this taxation year, attach a statement giving details.	☒	☐
6. Did the trust borrow money, or incur a debt, in a non-arm's length transaction since June 18, 1971? If yes, state the year, and if during this taxation year, attach a statement showing the amount of the loan, the lender's name, and the lender's relationship to beneficiaries.	☒	☐
7. Was the trust, in the previous taxation year, covered by an election to defer the deemed realization day (Form T1015)? If yes, and the trust did not have at least one exempt beneficiary throughout the year, state the date of death of the last exempt beneficiary, or the date the last exempt beneficiary no longer had an interest in the trust.	☒	☐
8. Does the will, trust document, or court order require the payment of trust income to beneficiaries?	☒	☐
9. Did the trust designate, under subsection 104(13.1) or (13.2), any portion of a beneficiary's income to be retained in the trust?	☒	☐
10. In which official language do you want to receive correspondence?	English ☒	French ☐

EXHIBIT 24, PAGE 2: INCOME TAX RETURN—ESTATE'S RETURN

Step 4 Calculating taxable income

Net Income of trust (from line 50 on page 2) 27,133,66 50

Deductions to arrive at taxable income

Non-capital losses of other years (see guide, line 51) .... 51 •

Net capital losses of other years (see guide, line 52) .... 52 •

Capital gains deduction for resident spousal trust only (from Schedule 5, line 525) .... 53 •

Other deductions to arrive at taxable income (specify) (see guide, line 54) 54 •

Add lines 51 to 54 inclusive. ▶ 55

Subtract line 55 from line 50. This is the trust's **taxable income.**
(If the amount is greater than zero, enter the amount at line 56, and on Schedule 11 at line 1101 or 1107.
If the amount is zero or negative, enter "0" at line 56, and enter the actual amount on Schedule 12 at line 1221 for minimum tax.) 27,133,66 56 •

(Deductions from net income (see guide, lines 51 to 54))

Step 5 Summary of tax and credits

Tax Federal tax payable (from Schedule 11, line 1129, or Schedule 12, line 1255) .... 4,600,03 81 •

Provincial or territorial tax payable (from Schedule 13 or 14) .... 2,657,30 82 •

Part XII.2 tax payable (from Schedule 10, line 1008) .... 83 •

Add lines 81 to 83 inclusive. **Total taxes payable** 7,257,33 ▶ 7,257,33 84 •

Credits Tax paid by instalments .... 85 •

Total tax deducted as shown on information slips .... 86 •

Refundable Quebec abatement (from Schedule 11, line 1130, or Schedule 12, line 1256) .. 87 •

Refundable investment tax credit (Form T2038(IND)) .... 88 •

Capital gains refund (from Form T184, mutual fund trust only) .... 89 •

Part XII.2 tax credit (from T3 slip, box 38) .... 90 •

Refundable Northwest Territories tax credit .... 91 •

Add lines 85 to 91 inclusive. **Total credits** ▶ 7,257,33 93

Subtract line 93 from line 84. **Balance owing or refund** 7,257,33 94
We do not refund or charge a difference of less than $2.

Amount enclosed 7,257,33 95
Payment: Attach a cheque or money order, payable to the Receiver General. Do not mail cash.

Refund code ☐ 100

Name of person or company (other than trustee, executor, or administrator) who prepared this return.	**Certification**
	I, (print name) MARY FRASER
Address in full	certify that the information given in this T3 return and in any documents attached is, to the best of my knowledge, correct, complete, and fully discloses the income from all sources.
	Mary Fraser
	Signature of authorized person
Postal code / Telephone ( )	EXECUTOR
	Position or title
Privacy Act personal information bank number RCT/P-PU-015	Date MARCH 5 19 97

The material on this form is condensed from the *Income Tax Act and Regulations*, which contain the terms of the law on which the tax is determined.

Printed in Canada

Ce formulaire existe aussi en français

EXHIBIT 25: CLEARANCE CERTIFICATE RECEIVED

Revenue Canada
Customs, Excise and Taxation

Revenu Canada
Accise, Douanes et Impôt

710631 TX21-A
Rev. 93

MARY ANN FRASER, EXECUTOR
937 CRICHTON AVENUE
DARTMOUTH, N. S.
B3A 4T7

DISTRICT TAXATION OFFICE:
BUREAU DE DISTRICT D'IMPÔT :

HALIFAX, N.S.

DATE   **97-05-13**

• ANY ALTERATION OR ERASURE RENDERS
THIS CERTIFICATE NULL AND VOID

• TOUS CHANGEMENTS OU RATURES RENDENT LE
PRÉSENT CERTIFICAT NUL ET DE NUL EFFET

CLEARANCE CERTIFICATE
(To date of death)

This is to certify that all amounts for which the taxpayer named below is liable and for the payment of which you may reasonably be expected to become liable in your capacity as the responsible representative of the taxpayer for the period ending with date of death and any preceding taxation year under the provisions of the Income War Tax Act; the 1948 Income Tax Act; the Income Tax Act; the Excess Profits Tax Act, 1940; the Canada Pension Plan; the Unemployment Insurance Act, 1971; the Petroleum and Gas Revenue Tax Act; the Income Tax Act – Newfoundland; the Income Tax Act – Prince Edward Island; the Income Tax Act – Nova Scotia; the Income Tax Act – New Brunswick; the Income Tax Act – Ontario; the Income Tax Act (Manitoba); the Income Tax Act – Saskatchewan; the Alberta Income Tax Act; the Income Tax Act – British Columbia; the Income Tax Act – Northwest Territories; or the Income Tax Act – Yukon Territory, have been paid or that security for the payment thereof has been accepted by the Minister.

CERTIFICAT DE DÉCHARGE
(À la date du décès)

La présente atteste que tous les montants dont un contribuable désigné ci-après est responsable et dont le paiement pourrait à bon droit vous incomber en votre qualité de représentant responsable du contribuable pour la période se terminant à la date du décès et pour n'importe quelle année d'imposition précédente, en vertu de la Loi de l'impôt de guerre sur le revenu, de la Loi de l'impôt sur le revenu (1948), de la Loi de l'impôt sur le revenu du Canada, de la Loi de 1940 sur la taxation des surplus de bénéfices, du Régime de pensions du Canada, de la Loi de 1971 sur l'assurance-chômage, de la Loi de l'impôt sur les revenus pétroliers, de la Loi de l'impôt sur le revenu du Nouveau-Brunswick et des lois dites « Income Tax Act » de Terre-Neuve, de l'Île-du-Prince-Édouard, de la Nouvelle-Écosse, de l'Ontario, du Manitoba, de la Saskatchewan, de l'Alberta, de la Colombie-Britannique, des Territoires du Nord-Ouest et du Territoire du Yukon, ont été payés ou que la garantie offerte pour leur paiement a été acceptée par le Ministre.

FRASER, JAMES ROBERT
DARTMOUTH, NOVA SCOTIA

DECEASED MAY 24, 1996

D. B. Gibson

D. B. Gibson

1- ORIGINAL

DIRECTOR-TAXATION / DIRECTEUR DE L'IMPÔT
DEPARTMENT OF NATIONAL REVENUE, TAXATION – MINISTÈRE DU REVENU NATIONAL, IMPÔT

PROVINCE OF NOVA SCOTIA)   **IN THE COURT OF PROBATE**
                                   In the estate of James Robert
COUNTY OF HALIFAX   ) Fraser, deceased.

TO HER HONOUR, Susan E. Cole, Registrar of the Court of Probate for the County of Halifax.

THE PETITION of Mary Ann Fraser, of Dartmouth, in the County of Halifax, Province of Nova Scotia, Executrix of the estate of James Robert Fraser, in his lifetime of Dartmouth, in the County of Halifax, aforesaid.

HUMBLY SHOWETH

1.   THAT James Robert Fraser, late of Dartmouth, Nova Scotia aforesaid, died on or about the 24th day of May, 1996, made his last will and testament wherein there was named Mary Ann Fraser, Executor.

2.   THAT probate of the estate of the said James Robert Fraser was granted to your petitioner by the Honourable Court on the 20th day of June, 1996, and an advertisement, a copy of which is annexed hereto and market Exhibit "A", was inserted in The Royal Gazette first on the 26th day of June, 1996, and continued therein for the period required by law.

3.   THAT your petitioner has caused to be filed in the Registry of this Honourable Court an inventory and valuation of the real and personal property of the deceased.

4.   THAT your petitioner prays for a day to be appointed for the auditing and passing of her account herein and further prays that a citation be issued to the heirs, creditors, legatees, next of kin and all persons in any way interested in the estate of the said James Robert Fraser calling on them to attend the adjudication of the claims of the creditors and other persons, the taking of the accounts of the said executrix and the final settlement and distribution of the said estate according to law.

AS IN DUTY BOUND your petitioner will ever pray.

DATED at Dartmouth, Nova Scotia, this 27th day of May, 1997

Mary A. Fraser.

EXHIBIT 26B: AFFIDAVIT ATTACHED TO PETITION TO CLOSE ESTATE
(REFER TO SECTION 70, NOVA SCOTIA PROBATE ACT)

Province of Nova Scotia	)	**In the Court of Probate**
County of Halifax	)	**In the estate of James Robert Fraser, deceased**

I, Mary Ann Fraser, make oath and say:

1.   **THAT** I am Mary Ann Fraser, the petitioner in the foregoing petition and have signed the same.

2.   **THAT** the facts set out in the annexed petition are true and correct.

Sworn before me at Dartmouth,
in the County of Halifax,
this ..9.7..day of May,
1997

....
A Barrister of the Supreme
     Court of Nova Scotia

Mary A Fraser
Mary Ann Fraser

EXHIBIT 27: LETTER TO REGISTRAR WITH DOCUMENTS

937 Crichton Avenue
Dartmouth, N. S.
B3A 4T7

Phone 469-5662

May 28, 1997

Ms. Susan E. Cole, Registrar
Probate Court, County of Halifax
1690 Hollis Street
Halifax, Nova Scotia
B3K 4G6

Dear Ms. Cole:

Estate of James Robert Fraser
Number 53694

Enclosed is my petition for a citation to close the estate on July 15th at 10.00 a.m..
Four copies of the citation are included for your use.

There three residual beneficiaries. Please provide me with three completed copies of the citation and I will give one to each of them.

Yours truly,

Mary A. Fraser.

Mary Ann Fraser
Executrix

PROVINCE OF NOVA SCOTIA)　　**IN THE COURT OF PROBATE**
　　　　　　　　　　　　　　　　　　In the estate of James Robert
COUNTY OF HALIFAX 　　　　　 **)** 　　**Fraser, deceased.**

TO the heirs, creditors, legatees, next-of-kin and all persons interested in the estate of James Robert Fraser late of Dartmouth, in the County of Halifax, aforesaid, deceased.

WHEREAS Mary Ann Fraser, executrix of the estate of the said deceased, has presented her petition praying that a day may be fixed for the passing of the executrix's accounts as such and for the final settlement of the said estate.

YOU ARE THEREFORE ENTITLED to appear before the Court of Probate at suite 910, 9th floor, The Centennial Building, 1660 Hollis Street, Halifax, Nova Scotia, on Tuesday, the 15th day of July, 1997, at 10.00 o'clock in the forenoon, to attend the adjudication of the claims of creditors or other persons, if any, the taking of the accounts of the executrix, Mary Ann Fraser, and the distribution of the estate according to law and to show cause, if any you have, why said account should not be so passed and said estate finally settled.

GIVEN under the seal of the said Court at Halifax, Nova Scotia, this 28th day of May, 1997.

Susan E. Cole

REGISTRAR
SUSAN E. COLE

EXHIBIT 29: LETTER TO ROYAL GAZETTE

937 Crichton Avenue
Dartmouth, N. S.
B3A 4T7

Phone 469-5662

May 28, 1997

The Royal Gazette
Department of Justice
5151 Terminal Road
Halifax, Nova Scotia
B3J 2L6

ESTATE OF JAMES ROBERT FRASER

The citation to close the above estate on July 15th has been issued. Please publish the required Notice:

ESTATE OF:

Date of Closing	Fraser, James Robert
	Dartmouth, Halifax County
	July 15-96-10.00 a.m. DST
Place of Closing	Court of Probate
	Centennial Building
	Halifax
Registrar	Susan E. Cole

A copy of the citation is presented for your examination. Please return it .

Enclosed is a cheque for $16.05 in payment.

Yours truly,

Mary A. Fraser

Mary Ann Fraser
Executrix

EXHIBIT 30: ROYAL GAZETTE EXCERPT

| 2870 | THE ROYAL GAZETTE | Wednesday, June 4, 1997 |

CITATION NOTICES

To the heirs, creditors, legates, next of kin and persons in any way interested in any of the undernoted estates WHEREAS petition has been presented by the representative or representatives of the estate, praying that a day may be fixed for the passing of their accounts as such representative for a partial or full settlement of said estates. You are therefore entitled to appear before the Court of Probate at the time and place set out below to attend the adjudication of the claims of the creditors, or other persons, if any, the taking of the said accounts and the distribution of the estate according to law and to show cause, if you have any, why the estate should not be passed and the estate partially or finally closed.

CITATION NOTICES BEING PUBLISHED FOR THE FIRST TIME

ESTATE OF: Date of Closing	Place of Closing at the Court of Probate	Registrar or Deputy Registrar and Date of First Insertion
BACON, Reverend Robert Leonard Amherst, Cumberland County September 4-96 - 10:00 a.m. DST	Court House Amherst	W. B. Fairbanks July 17-96 - (5iss)
BURGOYNE, Percy Guilford Springfield, Annapolis County August 21-96 - 11:00 a.m. DST	Court House Annapolis Royal	Lynn M. Durkee July 17-96 - (5iss)
CARTER, Reginald Morton Brookfield, Colchester County August 22-96 - 11:00 a.m. DST	Court House Truro	H. K. Starratt July 17-96 - (5iss)
FRASER, James Robert Dartmouth, Halifax County July 15-97 - 10.00 a.m.DST	Centennial Building Halifax	Susan E. Cole June 4-97 - (5iss)
FISHER, Arlene M. Truro, Colchester County August 19-96 - 11:00 a.m. DST	Court House Truro	H. K. Starratt July 17-96 - (5iss)
HENDERSON, Colleen Christy Halifax, Halifax County August 20-96 - 2:30 p.m. DST	Centennial Building Halifax	Sharron M. Grant July 17-96 - (5iss)
HENDERSON, Hugh Oswald Halifax, Halifax County August 20-96 - 2:00 p.m. DST	Centennial Building Halifax	Sharron M. Grant July 17-96 - (5iss)
HIRTLE, Ottis William Hemford, Lunenburg County August 19-96 - 10:00 a.m. DST	Court House Lunenburg	Armenia P. Corkum July 17-96 - (5iss)
LEVICK, Joseph Austin Halifax, Halifax County September 25-96 - 10:00 a.m. DST	Centennial Building Halifax	Geraldine Ernst July 17-96 - (5iss)
MacLEAN, Mary Jane Sydney, Cape Breton County August 27-96 - 2:00 p.m. DST	Harbour Place Sydney	Shauna L. Wilson July 17-96 - (5iss)

EXHIBIT 31, PAGE 1: EXECUTOR'S FINAL ACCOUNT STATEMENT

IN THE ESTATE OF JAMES ROBERT FRASER, DECEASED

FINAL ACCOUNT OF
MARY ANN FRASER, EXECUTRIX

SUMMARY

INVENTORY

REAL PROPERTY	144,760.00
PERSONAL PROPERTY	256,130.96

Adjustments to Inventory -

Additions

Deductions	-133.58
Adjusted Inventory Value	**400,757.38**
Income Receipts Schedule "A"	36,874.39
TOTAL VALUE	437,631.77
Less value of realty devised direct to beneficiary	144,760.00
VALUE ADMISTERED BY EXECUTOR	**292,871.77**

DISBURSEMENTS

Disbursements per Schedule "B"	237,662.36
Assets distributed per Schedule "C"	22,160.00
BALANCE ON HAND BEFORE CLOSING	**33,049.41**

CLOSING EXPENSES

Registrar of Probate - Fees on Closing	$	$632.00
Executor's or Administrator's Commission	$	0
Solicitor's Fees & Disbursements*	$	0.00
BALANCE FOR DISTRIBUTION..................		**$32,417.41**
Reserve is indicated, on page 4		500.00
Attested claims	$	-

*Solicitor's Disbursements - see Schedule "D" (Record Only)   nil

EXHIBIT 31. PAGE 2: EXECUTOR'S FINAL ACCOUNT STATEMENT

ESTATE OF JAMES ROBERT FRASER

SCHEDULE "A" - INCOME RECEIPTS

Personal Property	INVENTORY	INCOME	VALUE
Bank and broker accounts	26,257.18	523.14	26,780.32
Investments	171,725.00	1,825.00	173,550.00
Investments capital gains		34,020.00	34,020.00
Canada Savings Bonds	25,843.75	506.25	26,350.00
Vehicles	22,160.00	0.00	22,160.00
Accounts receivable	7,020.03	0.00	7,020.03
Life insurance	3,125.00	0.00	3,125.00
TOTALS	**256,130.96**	**36,874.39**	**293,005.35**

Adjustments to Inventory

Additions -

	0.00		0.00
Deductions -			
Bank account #3461-7	-133.58		-133.58
(May 24 amount overstated)			

Total personal property	**255,997.38**	**36,874.39**	**292,871.77**

ESTATE OF JAMES ROBERT FRASER

INCOME FOR ESTATE - SCHEDULE "A" SUPPLEMENTARY

Bank and broker accounts

1996

June 27 Bank of Montreal GIC interest	24.39
30 Bank of Nova Scotia interest on Estate a/c	1.15
July 31 Bank of Nova Scotia interest on Estate a/c	22.82
Aug. 5 Acadian Investments interest on a/c	13.98
31 Bank of Nova Scotia interest	34.89
Sep. 30 Bank of Nova Scotia interest	35.07
Oct. 31 Bank of Nova Scotia interest	37.90
Nov. 30 Bank of Nova Scotia interest	54.10
Dec. 31 Bank of Nova Scotia interest	54.21

1997

Jan. 31 Bank of Nova Scotia interest	54.97
Feb. 28 Bank of Nova Scotia interest	55.20
Mar. 31 Bank of Nova Scotia interest	51.08
Apr. 30 Bank of Nova Scotia interest	41.67
May 31 Bank of Nova Scotia interest	41.71

Total from bank and broker accounts   **$523.14**

INVESTMENTS INCOME

1996

July 26 Dividend on 1,000 shs Bank of Nova Scotia	340.00
Aug. 5 Dividends collected by Acadian Investments	945.00
15 Dividend on 1,000 shs Nova Scotia Power	200.00
Oct. 26 Dividend on 1,000 shs Bank of Nova Scotia	340.00

TOTAL INVESTMENT INCOME   **1,825.00**

Investments capital gains

Investment	May 24 value	Sale proceeds	Gain
500 shs Air Canada	2,125.00	2,370.00	245.00
2,000 shs Canadian Pacific	48,500.00	64,050.00	15,550.00
2,000 shs Maritime Tel & Tel	42,000.00	43,650.00	1,650.00
500 Shs Nor Tel	32,750.00	41,275.00	8,525.00
1,000 shs Bank Nova Scotia	32,500.00	39,750.00	7,250.00
10,000 shs Menora Resour.	2,600.00	1,325.00	-1,275.00
1,000 shs Nova Scotia Power	11,250.00	13,325.00	2,075.00
Total capital gains	**171,725.00**	**205,745.00**	**34,020.00**

Canada Savings Bonds:

INCOME FROM CANADA SAVINGS BONDS
Nov. 1/96 Interest paid $1,350. less May 24 accrual   **506.25**

EXHIBIT 31. PAGE 4: EXECUTOR'S FINAL ACCOUNT STATEMENT

ESTATE OF JAMES ROBERT FRASER

SCHEDULE "B" - DISBURSEMENTS

ACCOUNT

1996

1	Registrar of Probate	Fee	1,050.00
2	Royal Gazette	Notice	32.10
3	City Funeral Home Ltd.	Funeral	5,566.50
4	Sackville Cemetery Inc.	Burial plot	1,500.00
5	County of Lunenburg	Cottage taxes	246.00
6	Rotary Club of Dartmouth	Bequest	500.00
7	Church of the HolySpirit	Bequest	500.00
8	Elizabeth Wilson in trust	Bequest for Joanne	5,000.00
9	Elizabeth Wilson in trust	Bequest for Stanley	5,000.00
10	Richard J. Clarke, Q.C.	Documents preparation	214.00
11	Bank of Montreal Martercard	Deceased's account	697.60
12	Vacation Real Estate Ltd.	Cottage appraisal	100.00
13	Registry of Motor Vehicles	Licences for two cars.	222.00
14	Richard J. Clarke, Q.C.	Transfer ownership of Chester Basin property	342.67
15	Rigistrar of Probate	Additional fee	105.00
16	Louis Belliveau	Inventory appraisal	75.00
17	Peter Wilford	Inventory appraisal	75.00
18	Richard J. Clarke,Q.C.	Inventory appraisement documents	65.00
19	Hilltop Monuments Ltd.	Monument for cemetery	2,139.00
19	Revenue Canada	Income tax - May 24,1996	26,259.11
20	Elizabeth Joanne Wilson	Partial distribution	45,000.00
21	Christopher Robert Fraser	Partial distribution	45,000.00
22	Mary Ann Fraser	Partial distribution	90,000.00
23	Peter Wilford	Accounting services	200.00

1997

24	Revenue Canada	Estate income tax 12/31/96	7,257.33
25	Royal Gazette	Estate closing notice	16.05

RESERVE FOR OUTSTANDING ACCOUNTS:

Richard J. Clarke, Q.C. for document preparation		300.00
Peter Wilford for accounting services		200.00

TOTAL   237,662.36

ESTATE OF JAMES ROBERT FRASER

SCHEDULE "C" - ASSETS DISTRIBUTED

Type of asset	TO	AMOUNT
Real property- cottage	Christopher Robert Fraser	144,760.00
Personal property - car	Mary Ann Fraser	17,600.00
Personal property - car	Elizabeth Joanne Wilson	4,560.00
Total of personal property		22,160.00

937 Crichton Avenue
Dartmouth, N. S.
B3A 4T7

June 5, 1997   **REGISTERED MAIL**

Mrs Elizabeth Wilson
26 Humber Street
Halifax, N. S.
B6K 4M7

Dear Elizabeth: **ESTATE OF JAMES ROBERT FRASER**

This letter is to inform you that I have an appointment with the registrar of Probate to close your father's estate on July 15th, at 10.00 a.m.. The Court of Probate is located on the 9th floor, Centennial Building, 1660 Hollis Street, Halifax.

A copy of my account recording administration of estate assets has been prepared and is enclosed as well as the registrar of Probate's Citation to Close the estate. If you have any questions about these items, please do not hesitate to ask them.

I am sending a letter similar to this to Christopher and hope all three of us can attend the closing. That is when the registrar will hopefully approve and pass my account. I can pick you up on my way to court if you would like me to. Please let me know.

I do not intend to ask to be paid an executor's fee because such a fee would be income and subject to tax. The residue after closing will be a bit larger by my not taking a fee which will result in all three of us receiving a bit more when payout cheques are issued. My net after paying tax on a fee would have me end up with not much more money left in my hands than I would have by not taking an executor's fee; collectively as a family, I see no need to give any more of Jim's money to Revenue Canada than we have to. They have already taken enough.

With love,

Mary A Fraser

Mary Ann Fraser
Executrix

EXHIBIT 33: EXECUTOR'S AFFIDAVIT REGARDING CLOSING

PROVINCE OF NOVA SCOTIA	)	In the Court of Probate
COUNTY OF HALIFAX	)	In the estate of James
		Robert Fraser, deceased

I, Mary Ann Fraser of Dartmouth, in the County of Halifax, Province of Nova Scotia, make oath and say as follows;

1.   Letters of Probate were granted in the estate of James Robert Fraser, of Dartmouth, in the County of Halifax, Province of Nova Scotia, deceased, by this Honourable Court, on the 20th day of June, A.D., 1996:

2.   I did cause an advertisement to be inserted in The Royal Gazette for a period of six months beginning the 26th day of June, A.D., 1996, calling all persons who have any demands upon the estate of the deceased to exhibit such demands within six months from the date of the advertisement as is evidenced by the said advertisement, a true copy of which is attached hereto marked Schedule "A";

3.   The Citation to Close herein issued the 28th day of May, 1997, was served by mailing a true copy thereof by registered mail, postage prepaid, on the 5th day of June, A.D., 1997 to the following:

Mrs. Elizabeth Joanne Wilson	Mr. Christopher R. Fraser
26 Humber Street	1647 Summer Street
Halifax, N.S.	Halifax, N.S.
B6K 4M7	B7K 2H7

A true copy of the Registration Receipts is produced herewith marked Schedule "B" and is attached to this Affidavit.

Sworn before me at Dartmouth,
 in the County of Halifax,
 Province of Nova Scotia,
this ...26.th day .June,
1997

_____
A Barrister of the Supreme
Court of Nova Scotia

_____
Mary Ann Fraser

PROVINCE OF NOVA SCOTIA   )   **In the Court of Probate**
COUNTY OF HALIFAX   )   **In the estate of James**
                                           Robert Fraser, deceased

I, Mary Ann Fraser of Dartmouth, in the County of Halifax, Province of Nova Scotia, make oath and say:

1.   That I am Mary Ann Fraser the executrix of the estate of the above-named deceased.

2.   That the foregoing contains a true and correct account of the dealings of the executrix of the said estate, and in said account all assets and liabilities of the said estate are correctly shown and all bills known to me have been paid.

Sworn before me at Halifax,
 in the County of Halifax,
this ..15.th. day .July,
1997

Mary A. Fraser.
Mary Ann Fraser

Susan E. Pole
Registrar of Probate

EXHIBIT 35: LETTER TO REGISTRAR FOR CLOSING

937 Crichton Avenue
Dartmouth, N. S.
B3A 4T7

Phone 469-5662

June 23, 1997

Mrs. Susan E. Cole, Registrar
Probate Court, County of Halifax
1690 Hollis Street
Halifax, Novs Scotia
B3K 4G6

Dear Mrs. Cole

Estate of James Robert Fraser
No. 53694 closing on July 15th, 1997

Enclosed are the following documents for the closing:

Executrix's affidavit

Executrix's final account

Final Decree in duplicate

A photocopy of Revenue Canada's Clearance Certificate is attached.

Yours truly,

Mary Ann Fraser
Executrix

PROVINCE OF NOVA SCOTIA)   IN THE COURT OF PROBATE
COUNTY OF HALIFAX   )

IN THE MATTER OF the estate of James Robert Fraser
- and -
IN THE MATTER OF the passing and allowance of the account
of Mary Ann Fraser

WHEREAS Mary Ann Fraser, executrix or of the estate of James Robert Fraser having made an application for a final closing of the estate of the said deceased, the usual citation thereupon issued and the customary orders were made as to notice to parties interested to attend, and said citation was made returnable before us at the Registry of our said Court on Tuesday the 15th day of July A.D., 1997 at 10.00 o'clock in the forenoon;

AND WHEREAS at the Court of Probate for the County of Halifax aforesaid, duly holden on the 15th day of July A.D., 1997, at the place aforesaid, and at the same hour of 10.00 o'clock in the forenoon, we were attended by Mary Ann Fraser executrix of the said estate, together with vouchers in support thereof, and we then proceeded to the examination of the said account;

AND WHEREAS we have now made full, due and careful examination of the said account, and have compared the same with said vouchers, as also with the inventory on file in the said Registry in said estate, and with all papers and proceedings filed therein relevant to the matter of the accounting so had before us, and have after such examination and on full investigation and upon all charges and expenses attendant on the settlement of the said estate having been taxed and allowed and entered on said account, found the said account correct and satisfactory, the same being further verified by the oath thereon of the said executor and showing a balance remaining to the credit of the said estate to the value of $32,417.41 as shown by the said account:

IT IS THEREFORE HEREBY ORDERED, ADJUDGED AND DECREED that the said account be allowed and finally passed as a full and final accounting and the said account is hereby allowed and passed accordingly.

AND IT IS FURTHER ORDERED AND DECREED that Mary Ann Fraser executrix of the said estate, doth dispose of and distribute the said assets to the person or persons, at the time or times and in the manner set out in the said Last Will and that the said executrix on making such distribution doth in all respects conform to the terms and conditions of the said will.

DECREED at Halifax in the County of Halifax, under the seal of the said Court this 15th day of July A. D., 1997.

Susan E. Cole

REGISTRAR OF PROBATE

CODICIL

I , **JAMES ROBERT FRASER**, of Dartmouth, in the County of Halifax, Province of Nova Scotia make this Codicil to my Last Will and Testament dated the 25th day of November, 1993:

I **REVOKE** the appointment of my wife MARY ANN FRASER to be the executor of my Will, and in her place and stead appoint my brother George Trombone Fraser to be my executor and failing him my son Christopher Robert Fraser and my daughter Elizabeth Jane Wilson are to be joint executors in his place.

IN TESTIMONY WHEREOF I have subscribed my name this _____ day of _____ A.D., 199_.

Signed by James Robert Fraser,
the Testator, in the presence
of us both present at the same
time, who at his request, and in the
presence of each other have
hereto subscribed our names as
witnesses.

_____
Name..
Address ....
          ....
Occupation ....

                                        _____
                                        JAMES ROBERT FRASER

_____
Name..... ....
Address...
....
Occupation ....

TO MY FRIENDS, MY PHYSICIAN, MY LAWYER
AND OTHERS WHOM IT MAY CONCERN

Death is as much a reality as birth, growth and old age - it is the one certainty of life. If the time comes when I can no longer take part in decisions for my own future, let this stand as an expression of my wishes and directions, while I am still of sound mind.

If at such a time the situation should arise in which there is no reasonable expectation of my recovery from extreme physical or mental disability, I direct that I be allowed to die and not be kept alive by medications, artificial means or "heroic measures". I do however ask that medication be mercifully administered to me to alleviate suffering even though this may shorten my remaining life.

This statement is made after careful consideration and is in accordance with my strong convictions and beliefs. I want the wishes and directions here expressed carried out to the extent permitted by law. Insofar as they are not legally enforceable, I hope that those to whom this Will is addressed will regard themselves as morally bound by these provisions.

Signed _____

Name _____

Date_____

Signed in the presence of:

Witness_____
Address

Witness_____
Address

EXHIBIT 39: MOTOR VEHICLE STATUATORY DECLARATION

Canada
Province of Nova Scotia
County of _____

Statutory Declaration

IN THE MATTER OF

The Estate of _____ .

late of, _____ , in the

County of _____ , Deceased.

— and —

The application for transfer of registration of a motor vehicle owned in his lifetime by the said Deceased.

I, _____ , of _____ .

in the County of _____ , Province of Nova Scotia do solemnly declare as follows:

1.   THAT I am the _____ of _____ , deceased, and

late of _____ , in the County of _____ , Province of Nova Scotia.

2.   THAT the said _____ , died intestate on or about

the _____ day of _____ , A.D., _____ , leaving your Declarant herein surviving him.

3.   THAT the net value of the said deceased's estate does not exceed Fifty Thousand Dollars ($50,000.00).

4.   THAT among the assets of the said deceased's estate were/was a motor vehicle(s) described as follows:

VIN/SERIAL NO. _____

MAKE: _____

YEAR: _____

Registered under License Plate Number _____ for the year _____ .

5.   THAT pursuant to Chapter 236 of the Revised Statutes of Nova Scotia, 1989, amendments thereto, being the "Intestate Succession Act", all of the said deceased's estate goes to your Declarant herein.

6.   THAT the funeral expenses of the said deceased as well as all other just debts of the said deceased have all been assumed by me and have been or will be paid by me.

7.   THAT the Registrar of Motor Vehicles is requested to permit the transfer of the said motor vehicle(s) to _____

_____ , your Declarant herein.

8.   THAT I further undertake to indemnify and render harmless the Registry of Motor Vehicles or the Department of Transportation and Communications or any other Department of the Government of the Province of Nova Scotia for any claims which may be made against it with respect to the title of the said motor vehicle(s).

9.   THAT this Declaration is made for the purposes of inducing the Registry of Motor Vehicles to grant registration of the said vehicle(s) to the

said _____ .

SWORN to at _____ .   )

in the County of _____ .   )

this _____ day of _____ . .   )

A.D., 19 _____ .   )   _____
                          Signature

_____
A Barrister or Commissioner of the Supreme Court of Nova Scotia

FORM SPE20
Rev. 05/90/12590

CANADA
PROVINCE OF NOVA SCOTIA
COUNTY OF KINGS

POWER OF ATTORNEY

        KNOW ALL MEN BY THESE PRESENTS that I, Joseph Rufus Burtt of the town of Kentville, County of Kings, Province of Nova Scotia, appoint David J. C. Nicholl of the city of Dartmouth, County of Halifax, Province of Nova Scotia, my attorney to act for me and in my name in relation to my estate, real and personal, in his absolute discretion and as full and effectually as I personally could,

        AND to sign, make and endorse my name to cheques, bills of exchange, promissory notes or orders for the payment of money, and to deliver the same to the person entitled, or if payable to me to deposit in any bank, trust company or other depository,

        AND to invest in mortgages, bonds, debentures, mutual funds, or any other securities, and to subscribe for, purchase, pledge, sell, and deal with such securities and to vote and act in respect thereof,

        AND to let, manage, improve, sell and deal in any manner whatsoever with my real estate,

        AND to demand from any person whatsoever may be due or owing or belonging to me,

        AND to settle, compromise, and adjust any account between me and any person,

        AND to make claims, demands, seizures, levies, attachments, and to institute, prosecute or defend any action or other legal process,

        AND to execute leases, assurances, discharges and agreements as may be required,

        AND to have access to any safety deposit box I may have in any bank, trust company or institution having safety deposit boxes, and to deposit therein or remove therefrom the contents thereof,

AND to employ agents or others to assist in the foregoing,

AND I grant my attorney power to substitute attorneys under him with the same powers.

AND I expressly exclude the operation of subsection (2) of section 59 of the Province of Nova Scotia Hospitals Act,

THIS POWER OF ATTORNEY may be exercised during any legal incapacity on my part. I hereby ratify and confirm whatsoever my attorney (or his substitutes) shall do or cause to be done by virtue of these presents whether before or after my death until notice of my death or revocation hereof becomes known to my attorney, and, on behalf of myself, my heirs and my executors, I agree to indemnify my attorney from and against any loss or exposure he may incur in connection herewith.

IN WITNESS whereof the party hereto hereunder set his hand and affixed his seal on this 24th day of June, A.D. 1993.

SIGNED, SEALED AND DELIVERED
  in the presence of:

Ruth King.

Joseph R Burtt
Joseph Rufus Burtt

PROVINCE OF NOVA SCOTIA
COUNTY OF HANTS

On this 7th day of July, A.D., 1993 , before me, _Ruth King_ the subscribing witness to the foregoing POWER OF ATTORNEY personally came and appeared, who, having been by me duly sworn, made oath and said that Joseph Rufus Burtt, one of the parties hereto, signed, sealed and delivered the same in her presence.

Samuel J. Smith
A Barrister of the Supreme Court of Nova Scotia

THE PUBLIC GUARDIAN AND TRUSTEE

Continuing Power of Attorney for Property

(Made in accordance with the Substitute Decisions Act, 1992)

1. I,_____revoke any previous continuing power of attorney
    (Print or type your full name here.)
    for property made by me and **APPOINT**:_____

    _____ to be my attorney(s) for property.
    (Print or type the name of the person or persons you appoint here.)

2. If you have named more than one attorney and you want them to have the authority to act separately,
    insert the words "jointly and severally" here:_____
    (This may be left blank.)

3. If the person(s) I have appointed, or any one of them, cannot or will not be my attorney because of
    refusal, resignation, death, mental incapacity, or removal by the court, **I SUBSTITUTE**: *(This may be
    left blank.)*

    _____

    to act as my attorney for property with the same authority as the person he or she is replacing.

4. I AUTHORIZE my attorney(s) for property to do on my behalf anything in respect of property that I
    could do if capable of managing property, except make a will, subject to the law and to any conditions or
    restrictions contained in this document. I confirm that he/she may do so even if I am mentally incapable.

5. **CONDITIONS AND RESTRICTIONS**
    Attach, sign, and date additional pages if required. *(This part may be left blank.)*

    _____

    _____

    _____

    _____

    _____

    _____

    _____

    _____

6. DATE OF EFFECTIVENESS

Unless otherwise stated in this document, this continuing power of attorney will come into effect on the date it is signed and witnessed.

7. COMPENSATION

Unless otherwise stated in this document, I authorize my attorney(s) to take annual compensation from my property in accordance with the fee scale prescribed by regulation for the compensation of attorneys for property made pursuant to Section 90 of the *Substitute Decisions Act, 1992.*

8. SIGNATURE:_____DATE:_____

(Sign your name in the presence of two witnesses.)

ADDRESS:_____

(Insert your full current address here.)

_____

9. WITNESS SIGNATURE

[Note: The following people cannot be witnesses: the attorney or his or her spouse or partner; the spouse, partner, or child of the person making the document, or someone that the person treats as his or her child; a person whose property is under guardianship or who has a guardian of the person; a person under the age of 18.]

Witness #1:   *Signature:* _____   *Print Name:* _____

Address: _____

_____   *Date:* _____

Witness #2:   *Signature:*_____   *Print Name:* _____

Address: _____

THE PUBLIC GUARDIAN AND TRUSTEE

Power of Attorney for Personal Care

(Made in accordance with the Substitute Decisions Act, 1992)

1. I,_____revoke any previous power of attorney for personal
    (Print or type your full name here)

    care made by me and **APPOINT**:_____
    (Print or type the name of the person or persons you appoint here)
    _____

    to be my attorney(s) for personal care in accordance with the *Substitute Decisions Act, 1992*.

    [Note: A person who provides health care, residential, social, training, or support services to the person giving this power of attorney for compensation may not act as his or her attorney unless that person is also his or her spouse, partner, or relative.]

2. If you have named more than one attorney and you want them to have the authority to act separately,
    insert the words "jointly and severally" here:

    _____
    (This may be left blank)

3. If the person(s) I have appointed, or any one of them, cannot or will not be my attorney because of
    refusal, resignation, death, mental incapacity, or removal by the Court, **I SUBSTITUTE:**

    _____
    (This may be left blank)

    to act as my attorney for personal care in the same manner and subject to the same authority as the
    person he or she is replacing.

4. I give my attorney(s) the **AUTHORITY** to make any personal care decision for me that I am mentally
    incapable of making for myself, including the giving or refusing of consent to any matter to which the
    Health Care Consent Act, 1996 applies, subject to the *Substitute Decisions Act, 1992*, and any instruc-
    tions, conditions or restrictions contained in this form.

EXHIBIT 42, PAGE 2: POWER OF ATTORNEY—PERSONAL CARE (ONTARIO)

5. INSTRUCTIONS, CONDITIONS and RESTRICTIONS

Attach, sign, and date additional pages if required. *(This part may be left blank.)*

_____

_____

_____

_____

_____

_____

_____

_____

6. SIGNATURE:_____DATE:_____

(Sign your name here, in the presence of two witnesses.)

ADDRESS: _____

(Insert your current address here.)

_____

7. WITNESS SIGNATURES

[Note: The following people cannot be witnesses: the attorney or his or her spouse or partner; the spouse, partner, or child of the person making the document, or someone that the person treats as his or her child; a person whose property is under guardianship or who has a guardian of the person; a person under the age of 18.]

Witness #1:   *Signature:_____   Print Name:* _____

Address: _____

_____   *Date:* _____

Witness #2:   *Signature:_____   Print Name:* _____

Address: _____

_____   *Date:* _____

RELEASE

THIS INDENTURE made this 12th day of August ,1997

BETWEEN:
                                                Elizabeth Joanne Wilson
          hereinafter called "the Releasor"
          OF THE FIRST PART

AND:
          Mary Ann Fraser, executrix and
          trustee of the estate of the late
          James Robert Fraser hereinafter
          called "the Trustee"
          OF THE SECOND PART

WHEREAS James Robert Fraser, late of the Dartmouth, Halifax Regional Municipality, in the County of Halifax, and Province of Nova Scotia, departed this life on or about the 24th day of May, 1996 having made his last will and testament bearing date 23rd day of November 1993. Probate thereof was granted to the said Mary Ann Fraser on the 20th day of June 1996;

AND WHEREAS the Releasor, being a beneficiary under the last will and testament of the said James Robert Fraser has examined the accounts of the said estate and the administration thereof which are now produced by the Trustee, a copy of said accounts is hereto annexed and marked "A", each page having been initialled by the Releasor;

AND WHEREAS the parties hereto have mutually agreed to settle the said estate without the expense of a formal closing and accounting, and the Releasor has agreed to release the Trustee from all further responsibility with respect to the estate of the late James Robert Fraser;

NOW THEREFORE THIS INDENTURE WITNESSETH the Releasor has found the said accounts, annexed hereto marked "A", to be accurate;

AND FURTHER the Releasor, in consideration of the premises and in further consideration of the assets to be delivered by the Trustee, does hereby remise, release, quit claim and forever discharge the Trustee, her successors and assigns, of and from all manner of actions, causes of actions, debts, dues, accounts, bonds, covenants, contracts, claims and demands whatsoever in connection with the estate which the Releasor, her executors, administrators, successors and assigns ever had or, at any time hereafter, can or may have, claim or demand against the Trustee in relation to or concerning the said estate.

IN WITNESS WHEREOF I have hereunto set my hand and seal on the day and year first written above.

SIGNED, SEALED AND DELIVERED
in the presence of:

_____
  Witness
  Address: _____

                              _____
                              Elizabeth Joanne Wilson, the Releasor

_____

TRUSTEE'S CERTIFICATE

I, Mary Ann Fraser, executrix and Trustee of the estate of James Robert Fraser hereby certify that my annexed FINAL ACCOUNT marked "A" is a true and correct accounting of estate assets, all bills known to me have been paid and all duties imposed on me as executrix of the last will and testament of the late James Robert Fraser have been fulfilled.

_____
Mary Ann Fraser, executrix and trustee

GLOSSARY
OF TERMS

Acts of civil status - Civil Code of Quebec states that the only acts of civil status are acts of birth, marriage, and death.

Administrator - An individual or institution appointed by a court to administer and settle the estate of a deceased person. In Ontario the name is Estate Trustee and in Quebec the name is Liquidator.

Affidavit - Includes a solemn declaration, a statutory declaration, and an agreed statement of facts, sworn to be true.

Assets - Property of every kind and nature owned by a person or organization.

Attestation Clause - The statement in a will that it has been signed by the testator in the presence of witnesses. Also called a testimoum clause.

Attorney - Does not necessarily mean a "lawyer;" it also can mean anyone legally appointed to act for another person. A power of attorney document gives the attorney (the donee) the power to sign and do business for and in the name of the donor.

Beneficiary - A person who receive gifts of any kind under the terms of a will; also, the heir to an intestacy.

Certificate of Appointment of Estate Trustee with a Will - Ontario name for Letters Testamentary.

Certificate of Appointment of Estate Trustee without a Will - Ontario name for document appointing the administrator of an intestate's estate.

Certificate of Probate - Document issued by a probate court recording that a will has been proved and probate granted.

Chattel - Any moveable property; e.g., a vehicle, boat, furniture, lawn mower, or golf clubs.

Codicil - A document executed by a testator for adding to, altering, explaining, or confirming a will previously made. It becomes part of the will, must identify the will and must be executed with the same formalities as a will. It does not require to be witnessed by the same people who witnessed the signing of the will.

Common law spouse - In British Columbia, a person who is united to another by a marriage that, although not a legal marriage, is valid by common law; or a person who has lived with another person as a spouse and been maintained by that other person for a period of not less than two years immediately before the other person's death.

Corporeal - Material, tangible.

Descendants - All persons who can trace their descent through a given ancestor.

Devises, bequests, legacies - A devise is a gift of real estate or interest therein, a bequest is a gift of personal property, and a legacy is a gift of a specific sum of money.

Donee - Person to whom a power of attorney is given.

Donor - Person who gives a power of attorney.

Enduring power of attorney - The donee's authority continues to be valid notwithstanding any mental infirmity of the donor.

Estate - The assets, right, title, or interest that a person has in any properties, and the liabilities.

Estate Trustee - Ontario term for executor or administrator.

Executor (m.) executrix (f.) - Person(s) or institution named in a will to administer an estate in accordance with the directions of the testator/testatrix as contained in the will.

Funeral - traditional - Body embalmed and buried in a cemetery.

Funeral - non traditional - Body cremated.

Formal will - The document made by a person to take effect upon his death, in which he appoints an executor to distribute his properties and states who are to be the recipients. When it is presented for probate, any codicils are to be presented with it.

Grant of Probate - Decree made by a court of probate confirming that the executor named in a will has the legal authority to administer the deceased's estate. Appropriate documents are issued and may be called "Letters Probate" as well as "Certificates of Probate."

Guardian - A person named to be legally responsible for someone else, including both minors and adults. A guardian of property can be appointed to look after an incapable person's property or finances. A guardian of the person can be appointed by the court to make decisions for personal care on behalf of an incapable person. In Quebec the term is tutor.

Heir-at-law - The person who has a legal right to assets because of a blood relationship to an ancestor who dies intestate, i.e., without a will.

Holograph will - A will written by the testator and signed by him or her. (Exceptions may be made where the testator could not write and had someone else write for him.) No witness is required when written by the testator. It is not valid in Nova Scotia, Prince Edward Island and British Columbia. In some jurisdictions, handwriting includes mouthwriting and toewriting. In Saskatchewan, a dying farmer pinned under his tractor wrote his will on the tractor, using his blood. The will was declared valid for probate.

Illegitimate/legitimate - With respect to children, refers to the legal status arising from the matrimonial status of the natural parents.

Interment - Another term for burial.

Inter vivos trust - Also known as a living trust, inter vivos trusts are created during the lifetime of the settlor.

Intestate - A person who dies without a will. A partial intestacy is created when a valid will does not dispose of the whole estate.

Irrevocable trust - A trust which the settlor cannot revoke.

Issue - All persons who have descended from a common ancestor. It is not limited to just one generation but includes children, grandchildren and great grandchildren, and so on. See Descendants.

Joint tenancy - The form of joint ownership of property in which the death of one joint owner immediately results in the transfer of ownership to the surviving joint owner or owners.

Jurisdiction - Authority relating to the administration of justice; authority; or the area over which the justice authority has legal powers. A judge appointed in one province does not have jurisdiction powers outside that province.

Lawyer's trust account - Lawyers are legally required to deposit all money belonging to their clients in banking accounts clearly designated as "trust accounts." They maintain at least two banking accounts, one "general" for their own funds, and one trust account. Any interest earnings on trust funds have to be apportioned to clients or a lawyer society.

Legacy - See Devises.

Legal Representative - An executor, administrator, liquidator, tutor or a judicial trustee of the estate of a deceased person, or, the guardian of a minor.

Legatee - Recipient of a legacy.

Letters of administration - A document issued by a court of probate to the personal representative of a person having died without a valid will and therefore intestate. The appointed administrator's duties are similar to those of an executor, except that they are carried out under intestate succession act requirements.

Letters Probate - The same as a Grant of Probate.

Letters Testamentary - A document issued by a court of probate in Nova Scotia with a copy of the will attached to it, certifying that the executor has been legally appointed to administer the estate.

Liquidator - Quebec term for an executor or administrator of an estate.

Living will - A document describing the medical treatment an individual wishes or does not wish to receive once that individual is no longer able to communicate with a physician.

Lunatic - In New Brunswick, a person mentally incompetent, either mentally handicapped or mentally ill.

Marker - A stone or bronze tablet that rests flush with the ground and identifies the grave.

Mental incompetence - The inability of a person to manage his or her affairs by reason of mental infirmity arising from age, disease, addiction, or other cause.

Military, mariners', fishermen's, Seamen's wills - Wills made by people working in such occupations who may be under the age of majority, away from their home for long periods, at times under life-threatening situations. While these wills may not meet normal probate and wills format requirements, provincial and territorial acts nevertheless make provision for such wills to be accepted for probate.

Monument - An upright stone, or sometimes a combination of stone and bronze standing above ground, which identifies a grave; a "tombstone".

Minor – A person who has not reached the age of majority which varies from 18 to 19 years of age in the provinces and territories. For estate inheritance purposes, some jurisdictions recognize an unborn child as a minor.

Notarial will (Quebec) - A will having special status, valid without being probated in Quebec.

Notaries Public - Lawyers appointed by governments.

Oath - includes a solemn affirmation and statutory declaration.

Personal representative - The executor of the will; temporary administrator of a deceased person's estate; someone appointed by letters under the seal of a court.

Personal property - All a person's belongings with the exception of real estate, i.e. land. This includes bank accounts, stocks and bonds, investments of every kind, art collections, and so on.

Petitioner - A person making an application to a court.

Power of attorney - A document in which someone (the "donor") gives another person (the "donee") the authority and power to sign documents in the donor's name. An enduring power of attorney is one that is not terminated by any mental incapacity or infirmity of the donor that occurs after it was executed. A power of attorney terminates when the donor dies.

Probate - The procedure whereby the will of a deceased person is proved by law and registered in the court to record that the administration of the deceased's estate has been granted to the executor(s) named in the will.

Proof in common form - Probate court procedure to prove a deceased person's will in ordinary cases. Generally the executor named in the will swears it is authentic and files affidavits requesting probate be granted, which it usually is.

Proof in solemn form - A more complicated probate court procedure to prove a deceased person's will. It is used when there is or is likely to be a dispute as to the validity of the will or disbursements under it.

Proof of death certificate - Issued either by the funeral home or the province's vital statistics office. It takes longer to obtain from the latter.

Property - Includes both real property (real estate) and personal property (any other assets).

Public trustee - Person appointed by a government to take control of the assets of deceased and other persons when no one else has that legal responsibility, or someone previously given the task has failed to fulfil such responsibilities.

Real property - Real estate, land including any interest in land such as a lease or right-of-way.

Residuary beneficiary - A person who receives a part or all of the residue of an estate.

Residue - That portion of an estate that is left after all debts, expenses, and legacies have been paid.

Revocable Trust - A trust which can be revoked by the person who created it.

Royal Gazette - A provincial government publication in which legal notices are placed. Not in use in Quebec.

Settlor - A person who establishes a Trust.

Spouse - Generally understood to be opposite sex couples in a married or living together relationship. However, British Columbia's Adult Guardianship Act defines "spouse" as a person who (a) is married to another person and not living separate and apart from the other person; or (b) is living with another person in a marriage-like relationship and, for the purposes of this act, the marriage or marriage-like relationship may be between members of the same sex.

Statute - An act of Parliament or provincial or territory legislature; law

Surety - A person who makes himself responsible for another's debts; a guarantor.

Swear - To attest that the facts in a document are true, before a lawyer, judge, notary, or other person legally appointed to take affidavits.

Tax Clearance Certificate - Issued by Revenue Canada on request, after all the deceased's income tax and any other taxes owing have been paid.

Tenancy in common - A form of joint ownership of property by two or more people, in equal or different proportions. Upon the death of one of them that person's share in the property becomes part of his estate and does not pass to the survivor(s).

Testamentary Letters - Document issued by a court of probate directing the disposition of a deceased's property.

Testamentary Trust - A trust set up by the will upon the death of the testator, containing the estate's properties and all receipts therefrom.

Testate - A deceased person who has left a valid will is said to have died testate.

Testator (m), testratrix (f) - The person who makes a will.

Testimoum clause - The final clause in a formal will.

Trust, trustee -The practice of a person or corporation holding and managing property on behalf of someone. For example, a testator in his or her will may direct his or her executor to hold certain property in trust for his or her infant children until they reach the age of majority, and that income earned from the property be paid to them for living expenses. Trust companies are frequently chosen to be trustees because of their reputation for permanency.

Tutor - Similar to guardian in provinces and territories other than Quebec. Quebec's Civil Code makes provision for parents in their wills to appoint tutors for minor children. Tutors can be appointed by a declaration filed with the public curator, among other processes.

Tutorship council - In Quebec, a group composed of up to three persons to supervise tutorship.

Urn - A container for the cremated remains of the deceased.

Witness - A persons present when the testator signed his or her will.

Will - Includes a testament, a codicil, or an appointment by will or any other testamentary disposition.

RESEARCH SOURCES

Chapter 11 contains the names of Provincial and Territorial Acts from which much of the information in this chapter was obtained.

Other sources include:

Copies of estate, intestate and guardianship documents which have been processed through Probate Courts of Nova Scotia and the Supreme Court of Nova Scotia.

Bank of Nova Scotia deceased customer estate guidance overview, April 1997.

Canadian Snowbird Association News, December 1997.

Everyone's Guide to the Law, Linda Silver Dranoff, 1997, Harper Collins Publishers Ltd. Toronto.

Financial Planning Guide, Norwich Union Life Insurance Company (Canada).

Nova Scotia Barrister's Society pamphlet, 1984 (revised).

Nova Scotia Probaie Law & Procedure, Vincent P. Allen, Q.C., 1993.

Ontario, The Public Guardian and Trustee, *Powers of Attorney* booklet by Ontario Ministry of the Attorney General, 1996.

Public Legal Education Society of Nova Scotia pamphlets, 1993.

Estate Planning, Wills and Executors, Royal Trust, 1996.